Business Tax

(Finance Act 2016)

Workbook

for assessments from January 2017

osborne BOOKS

/ / AUG 2017

Aubrey Penning
Bob Thomas

Published by Osborne Books Limited
Tel 01905 748071
Email books@osbornebooks.co.uk
Website www.osbornebooks.co.uk

Design by Laura Ingham

Printed by CPI Group (UK) Limited, Croydon, CR0 4YY, on environmentally friendly, acid-free paper from managed forests.

MIX
Paper from
responsible sources
FSC® C019777

British Library Cataloguing in Publication Data
A catalogue record for this book is available from the British Library

ISBN 978 1909173 934

Contents

Introduction

Chapter activities

Also available from Osborne Books...

Tutorials

Clear, explanatory books written
precisely to the specifications

  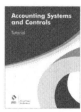 

   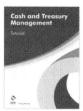 

Student Zone

Login to access your free ebooks and
interactive revision crosswords

Download **Osborne Books App** free from the App Store or Google Play Store
to view your ebooks online or offline on your mobile or tablet.

www.osbornebooks.co.uk

Introduction

Qualifications covered

This book has been written specifically to cover the Unit 'Business Tax' which is an optional Unit for the following qualifications:

AAT Professional Diploma in Accounting – Level 4

AAT Professional Diploma in Accounting at SCQF – Level 8

The book contains a clear text with worked examples and case studies, chapter summaries and key terms to help with revision. Each chapter concludes with a wide range of activities, many in the style of AAT computer based assessments.

Osborne Study and Revision Materials

The materials featured on the previous page are tailored to the needs of students studying this Unit and revising for the assessment. They include:

- **Tutorials:** paperback books with practice activities
- **Student Zone:** access to Osborne Books online resources
- **Osborne Books App:** Osborne Books ebooks for mobiles and tablets

Visit www.osbornebooks.co.uk for details of study and revision resources and access to online material.

Exams, Finance Acts and tax years

This book has been designed to include guidance and exercises based on Tax Year 2016/17 (Finance Act 2016). We understand that the AAT plan to assess this legislation from 1 January 2017 to 31 December 2017. Tutors and students are advised to check this with the AAT and ensure that they sit the correct computer based assessment.

Chapter activities

1 Introduction to business taxation

1.1 Which of the following statements are true and which are false?

	True	False
(a) A self employed taxpayer must pay Class 2 NIC, unless the 'small profits threshold' applies		
(b) Class 4 NIC is payable by the self employed only when drawings are over £8,060		
(c) Class 4 NIC is payable by the self employed when profits are over £8,060		
(d) Class 4 NIC is paid at the same time as income tax under self-assessment		
(e) Class 4 NIC is payable at 2% on profits over £43,000		

1.2 Using the following table, insert the details and dates relating to online returns and payment of tax.

	Period return relates to	Latest return submission date	Latest tax payment date
Corporation Tax			
Income Tax			

Select from the following:

- Tax year
- Financial year
- 12 months after end of tax year
- 12 months after end of chargeable accounting period
- 9 months and one day after end of chargeable accounting period
- 12 months after end of period that accounts are based on
- Chargeable accounting period
- 31 January following tax year
- 31 October following tax year

1.3

(a) A taxpayer has self employed income of £60,000 for the tax year 2016/17. The amount chargeable to NIC at 9% would be:

£ [   ]

(b) A taxpayer has self employed income of £45,000 for the tax year 2016/17. The amount of total Class 4 NIC payable would be:

£ [   ]

1.4 State whether each of the following is true or false.

	True	False
(a) A self employed individual's tax records relating to his business for 2016/17 need to be kept until 31 January 2023, or longer if an investigation is being carried out		
(b) HMRC has a right to visit premises to inspect records		
(c) Accountants must normally follow the rules of confidentiality, but there are exceptions		
(d) Where a practitioner has knowledge or suspicion that his client is money laundering, then he has a duty to inform the relevant person or authority		
(e) The AAT Code of Professional Ethics applies to AAT members, but not to AAT students		
(f) When an accountant is advising a client the greatest duty of care is to HMRC		

1.5 State the final submission dates for tax returns for the following businesses.

A sole trader with accounts made up to 31 March 2017	
A sole trader with accounts made up to 30 June 2017	
A limited company with accounts made up to 31 December 2016	

2 Corporation tax – trading profits

2.1 A limited company has the income and expenses as shown in the following table recorded in its statement of profit or loss. In order to calculate the adjusted trading profit, some items need to be added and some deducted from the net profit. Some items do not require any adjustment.

Analyse the income and expenses, by ticking the appropriate columns in the table.

	Add to net profit	Deduct from net profit	No adjustment required
Depreciation			
Discount received			
Directors' salaries			
Dividends received			
Rent receivable			
Rent payable			
Interest payable			
Advertising costs			
Entertaining customers			

2.2   River Limited has the following summarised statement of profit or loss.

	£	£
Sales		120,000
less cost of sales		35,000
gross profit		85,000
add gain on sale of non-current asset		12,000
		97,000
less expenses:		
administration expenses	18,000	
depreciation	13,000	
charitable payments (gift-aid)	2,000	
entertaining staff	5,000	
vehicle expenses	22,000	
		60,000
Net profit		37,000

Select the adjusted trading profit (before capital allowances) from the following:

(a)	£57,000	
(b)	£45,000	
(c)	£40,000	
(d)	£34,000	
(e)	£37,000	
(f)	£38,000	

2.3　State whether each of the following statements is true or false.

	True	False
(a) The basis of assessment for trading profits is the tax adjusted trading profits of the chargeable accounting period, prepared on an accruals basis		
(b) Lease rental payments for cars are never allowable as they are deemed to be capital expenditure		
(c) Interest payable on trade loans is not allowable		
(d) If a loan to an employee is written off, the amount is not an allowable deduction		
(e) Donations to political parties are an allowable expense		
(f) Employers' national insurance contributions are not an allowable deduction as they are effectively a form of taxation		
(g) Employees' parking fines incurred while on business are an allowable deduction		

2.4　If an accounting period is longer than 12 months, which of the following statements shows the correct approach?

(a)　Provided the accounting period is not more than 18 months long, the whole period can form one chargeable accounting period	
(b)　The capital allowances are calculated for the long accounting period and deducted from the adjusted trading profits for the long accounting period. This is then time-apportioned into two chargeable accounting periods	
(c)　It is illegal to prepare accounts for a limited company for more than 12 months, so the problem does not arise	
(d)　The trading profits for the long accounting period are time-apportioned into two periods before tax adjustments are carried out to each period's profit. Capital allowances are calculated for the long period and then time-apportioned, before being deducted from each period's adjusted profits	
(e)　The trading profits for the long period are adjusted for tax purposes (before capital allowances), and the result is time-apportioned into two chargeable accounting periods. Separate capital allowance computations are carried out for each chargeable accounting period, and then deducted from each of the adjusted trading profits	

2.5   A limited company has the following tax-adjusted results for years to 31 December 2015 and 2016:

	2015	2016
Trading Income	£50,000	£0
Income from Investments	£18,000	£15,000
Chargeable Gains	£0	£10,000

The company made a trading loss in 2016 of £81,000.

The company has no qualifying research and development expenditure.

What is the maximum amount of loss that could be set against the taxable total profits for 2015?

(a) £56,000	
(b) £68,000	
(c) £50,000	
(d) £66,000	
(e) £0	

3   Corporation tax – capital allowances

3.1   Analyse the following items into those that qualify as plant and machinery for capital allowance purposes, (under corporation tax) and those that do not, by ticking the appropriate column.

	Qualify	Do not qualify
Car for employee's private use		
Office furniture		
Capital expenditure on software		
Payments for vehicle on operating lease		
Vehicles bought on credit		
Buildings		
Equipment bought through hire purchase		

3.2   A company has a 12-month chargeable accounting period ending on 31/3/2017, with no written down values brought forward for capital allowance purposes. During the period the company purchased:

* A new low-emission car for £26,000

* A car with emissions of 180 g/km for £22,000

* Plant for £60,000

Calculate the maximum capital allowances that can be claimed, and insert the figures into the following sentences.

The AIA that can be claimed is £

The first year allowance that can be claimed at 100% is £

The writing down allowance that can be claimed at 18% is £

The writing down allowance that can be claimed at 8% is £

The total capital allowance that can be claimed is £

3.3 Analyse each of the following capital acquisitions into the relevant category by ticking the appropriate column.

	AIA (to limit)	Main pool	Special rate pool	100% FYA
Car emissions of 185 g/km				
Car emissions of 99 g/km				
Machinery				
Zero-emission goods vehicle				
Car emissions of 125 g/km				
Water-efficient plant				

3.4 State whether each of the following statements is true or false.

	True	False
(a) For a CAP of 9 months, the AIA for each acquisition that qualifies would be scaled down to 9/12 of its cost. For example, an asset bought for £20,000 would only be entitled to £15,000 AIA		
(b) For a CAP of 9 months, any writing down allowance would be scaled down to 9/12 of the equivalent amount for a 12 month period, but first year allowances and balancing allowances would not be affected		
(c) For a CAP of 9 months, any first year allowance would be scaled down to 9/12 of the equivalent amount for a 12 month period, but writing down allowances and balancing allowances would not be affected		
(d) For a CAP of 9 months the annual investment allowance (AIA) limit would be calculated by time-apportionment		
(e) For a CAP of 9 months the writing down allowance is unaffected		

3.5   A company has the following information regarding its non-current assets for a 12-month CAP, ending on 31/12/2016.

	£
Written down values brought forward:	
General (main) pool	120,000
Special rate pool	19,000
Additions:	
Machinery	60,000
New car for Sales Director (emissions 190 g/km)	35,000
Disposals:	
Machinery	5,000
Sales Director's car (special rate pool)	7,000

Calculate the maximum capital allowances for the CAP.

4   Corporation tax – chargeable gains

4.1   Select the appropriate disposal proceeds amount to be used in the chargeable gains computation of a limited company by ticking the appropriate column.

	Actual proceeds	Market value	£6,000	Zero
Sale of asset for £15,000 to Director who owns 80% of shares in company. Market value of asset is £35,000				
Gift of asset to unconnected individual (non-shareholder)				
Sale of asset to company employee (non-shareholder) at below market value				
Sale of chattel for £4,000 (its market value) that had originally cost £10,000				
Destruction of an uninsured asset during fire				
Sale of asset for £15,000 to Director who owns 10% of shares in company. Market value of asset is £35,000				
Shares owned in an unconnected company that have become worthless due to the company's liquidation				

4.2   Tousist Ltd sold an antique office desk for £10,000 in April 2016. This was bought for £3,500 in August 2000. The indexation factor from August 2000 to April 2016 was 0.533.

Complete the following computation:

Proceeds: £ _____

Cost: £ _____

Indexation allowance: £ _____

Gain: £ _____

Chattel restriction on gain: £ _____

State whether the chattel restriction will have any effect on the original gain.   YES / NO

4.3 Penfold Ltd bought 8,000 shares in Tempter Ltd for £19,500 in October 2001. A rights issue of 1 for 40 shares was bought in July 2003 for £1.80 per share. In April 2016, Penfold Ltd sold 6,000 of the shares for £4 per share.

Indexation factors were: October 2001 to July 2003: 0.114; July 2003 to April 2016: 0.442

What is the gain made on the share disposal?

	No. shares	Cost £	Indexed cost £

Proceeds	£
Indexed Cost	£
Gain	£

4.4 Treacle Ltd sold a 2 acre plot of land for £40,000 in April 2016. This was part of a 6 acre plot that was bought for £90,000 in August 2000. The 4 acres that were retained were valued at £60,000 at the time of the sale. The indexation factor from August 2000 to April 2016 was 0.533.

Complete the following computation:

Proceeds: £

Cost: £

Indexation allowance
(before restriction):   £

Gain or (Loss): £

4.5 Trapper Ltd sold a painting for £5,500 in April 2016. This was bought for £7,500 in August 2000. The indexation factor from August 2000 to April 2016 was 0.533.

Complete the following computation:

Proceeds: £

Cost: £

Indexation allowance: £

Gain or (Loss): £

5   Corporation tax – calculating the tax

5.1   Different types of losses can be relieved in different ways. From the list below, select one rule that can apply to each of the losses stated in the table.

Loss	Rules that can apply
Trading Loss	
Capital Loss	
Rental Loss	

Select from:

(a)   Set against current period taxable total profits (TTP), with any unused amount carried forward and set against future taxable total profits (TTP)

(b)   Set against chargeable gains of same CAP, with any unused loss set against taxable total profits (TTP) of current period

(c)   Set against chargeable gains of same CAP, with any unused loss set against chargeable gains of previous period

(d)   Set against current period taxable total profits (TTP), with any unused amount carried forward and set against future chargeable gains

(e)   Set against trading profits of following CAP

(f)   Set against chargeable gains of same CAP, with any unused loss set against chargeable gains of following period

5.2 Xenopus Limited has the following results for the year ended 30/9/2016:

Trading Profits	£1,350,000
Rental Income	£250,000
Chargeable Gains	£220,000
Dividends Received	£180,000

The company also has the following losses brought forward from the previous CAP:

Trade Losses	£130,000
Capital Losses	£50,000

Complete as far as possible the following extract from the CT600 Corporation Tax Return for Xenopus Limited:

Tax calculation
Turnover

145 Total turnover from trade £ · 0 0

150 Banks, building societies, insurance companies and other financial concerns –
put an 'X' in this box if you do not have a recognised turnover and have not made an entry in box 145

Income

155 Trading profits £ · 0 0

160 Trading losses brought forward claimed against profits £ · 0 0

165 Net trading profits – *box 155 minus box 160* £ · 0 0

170 Bank, building society or other interest, and profits from non-trading loan relationships £ · 0 0

172 Put an 'X' in box 172 if the figure in box 170 is net of carrying back a deficit from a later accounting period

175 Annual payments not otherwise charged to Corporation Tax and from which Income Tax has not been deducted £ · 0 0

Income *continued*

180	Non-exempt dividends or distributions from non–UK resident companies	£

185	Income from which Income Tax has been deducted	£

190	Income from a property business	£

195	Non-trading gains on intangible fixed assets	£

200	Tonnage Tax profits	£

205	Income not falling under any other heading	£

Chargeable gains

210	Gross chargeable gains	£

215	Allowable losses including losses brought forward	£

220	Net chargeable gains - *box 210 minus box 215*	£

Profits before deductions and reliefs

225	Losses brought forward against certain investment income	£

230	Non-trade deficits on loan relationships (including interest) and derivative contracts (financial instruments) brought forward	£

235	Profits before other deductions and reliefs – *net sum of boxes 165 to 205 and 220 minus sum of boxes 225 and 230*	£

5.3 State whether each of the following statements is true or false.

		True	False
(a)	Companies must inform HMRC within six months that they have started trading. The penalty for failing to notify is £3,000		
(b)	The flat penalty for failure to submit a Corporation Tax Return on time is £100 for up to three months late and £200 for over three months late. A percentage penalty based on the Corporation Tax can also apply		
(c)	Interest is charged on late payments (including instalments). The interest charged is an allowable deduction against non-trading interest		
(d)	Errors in tax returns caused by a lack of reasonable care can suffer a penalty of between 0% and 50% of the extra tax due		
(e)	Failure to keep records can result in a penalty of £3,000 per chargeable accounting period		
(f)	Errors in tax returns that are both deliberate and concealed are subject to a penalty of up to 100% of the extra tax due		
(g)	Records need to be kept for at least six years from the end of the accounting period		

6   Income tax – trading profits

6.1   From the following factors, tick those that are considered the 'badges of trade' which are used to determine whether an individual is trading.

	Badges of Trade
Reason for acquisition and sale of item(s)	
Whether individual enjoys carrying out the activity	
Whether there is a profit motive	
How long the individual has owned the item(s) before sale	
Whether the individual only sells via computer sites	
Whether any supplementary work is carried out on the item(s) before sale	
Whether the individual considers the activity to be his hobby	
How often the individual carries out similar transactions	
Whether the items bought and sold (the subject matter) are used personally by the individual before sale	

6.2   Analyse the following expenditure of a sole trader into those that are allowable deductions for tax purposes and those that are not, by ticking the appropriate column.

	Allowable expenditure	Non-allowable expenditure
Cost of sales		
Entertaining staff		
Fines for lawbreaking by business owner		
Gifts of food or drink to customers		
Trade bad debts written off		
Salary and NIC of business owner		
Depreciation		
Loss on sale of non-current assets		

6.3   Laura Little is a sole trader. Her business has the following statement of profit or loss:

	£	£
Turnover		1,256,000
Cost of sales		815,400
Gross profit		440,600
Wages and salaries	120,560	
Rent, rates and insurance	51,210	
Repairs to plant	8,615	
Advertising and entertaining	19,535	
Accountancy and legal costs	5,860	
Motor expenses	50,030	
Telephone and office costs	18,050	
Depreciation	22,020	
Other expenses	32,410	328,290
Net Profit		112,310

Notes:

1. Laura took goods from the business that cost £1,200 and would normally sell for £2,000. The cost is included in cost of sales.

2. Wages and salaries include:
	£
Laura Little	45,000
Laura's son, who works during the school holidays	28,000

3. Advertising and entertaining includes:
	£
Gifts to customers:	
Bottles of wine costing £12 each	2,400
400 mouse mats carrying the business's logo	600

4. Motor expenses include:
	£
Delivery van expenses	10,150
Laura's car expenses (used for business only)	5,900
Laura's son's car expenses (used only for private use)	3,800

5. Other expenses include:
	£
Cost of staff training	3,150
Increase in general bad debt provision	2,600

6. Capital allowances have already been calculated at £10,400

Complete the adjusted trading profits computation.

6.4 Mavis Deacon has a 12-month accounting period ending on 30/9/2016, with no written down values brought forward for capital allowance purposes. In January 2016 she purchased:

- A van with 20% private use for £18,000
- A car with emissions of 120 g/km and 40% private use for £20,000
- Machinery for £30,000

Calculate the maximum capital allowances that can be claimed, and insert the figures into the following sentences.

The AIA that can be claimed is £

The single asset pool writing down allowance that can be claimed is £

The special rate pool writing down allowance that can be claimed is £

The total capital allowance that can be claimed is £

The total written down value carried forward is £

6.5 A sole trader has the following tax-adjusted results for the tax years 2015/16 and 2016/17:

	2015/16	2016/17
Trading Profits	£20,000	£0
Other Income	£17,000	£28,000

The sole trader incurred a trading loss in 2016/17 of £44,000.

What is the maximum amount of the loss that could be set against the individual's income for 2015/16?

(a) £20,000	
(b) £37,000	
(c) £44,000	
(d) £16,000	
(e) £0	

7 Income tax – further issues

7.1 Clive started trading on 1 November 2014. He makes up his accounts to 31 December each year. The profits were calculated at:

	£
Period to 31 December 2014	16,000
Year to 31 December 2015	108,000
Year to 31 December 2016	92,000

(a) The tax year in which he started trading was (select one):

2012/13; 2013/14; 2014/15; 2015/16

(b) His taxable profits in his first tax year of trading were (select one):

£16,000; £43,000; £108,000; £124,000

(c) His taxable profits in his second tax year of trading were (select one):

£92,000; £97,000; £108,000; £124,000

(d) His taxable profits in his third tax year of trading were (select one):

£108,000; £124,000; £104,000; £92,000

(e) His overlap profits were £ [   ]

(f) His overlap profits are deducted (select one):

from his first year profits	
from the profits in the second year of trading	
from the profits in the third year of trading	
from the profits in the final year of trading, or on a change of accounting date	

7.2   An individual commences business as a sole trader on 1 February 2015. He makes his first set of accounts up to 30 April 2016, and thereafter to 30 April each year.

What is the basis period for the tax year 2015/16?

(a) 1 February 2015 to 30 April 2016	
(b) 1 May 2015 to 30 April 2016	
(c) 1 February 2015 to 31 January 2016	
(d) 6 April 2015 to 5 April 2016	
(e) 1 February 2015 to 5 April 2015	
(f) 1 February 2015 to 5 April 2016	

7.3   Pete and Heather have been in partnership for many years, running a fish smoking business, and sharing profits equally. They have always made their accounts up to 31 December each year.

On 1 September 2016, Ash joined the partnership and the profit sharing ratio was changed to 3:3:2 for Pete, Heather and Ash.

For the year ended 31 December 2016, the trading profit was £120,000.

(1)   Using the following table, calculate the division of profits between the partners for the accounting year ended 31 December 2016.

	Total	Pete	Heather	Ash
	£	£	£	£
1 Jan - 31 August 2016				
1 Sep - 31 Dec 2016				
Total				

(2)   What is the basis of assessment for 2016/17 for Ash?

(a) 1/9/2016 - 31/12/2016	
(b) 1/1/2016 - 31/12/2016	
(c) 1/9/2016 - 5/4/2017	
(d) 1/1/2017 - 5/4/2017	

7.4   Joe Salt's total income tax and Class 4 NIC for 2015/16 has been finalised as £11,600, all relating to his business as a sole trader. He made payments on account of £4,000 on each of 31 January 2016 and 31 July 2016 relating to 2015/16.

Using the following table, calculate the amounts of the payments that he needs to make on 31 January 2017 and 31 July 2017, assuming no claim to reduce payments is made.

		£
Payment on 31 January 2017	Balance of tax and NIC for 2015/16	
	Payment on account for 2016/17	
	Total	
Payment on 31 July 2017	Payment on account for 2016/17	

7.5   Deborah Baker commenced in business on 1 October 2016. She produced accounts for the year ended 30 September 2017, and the information from these accounts has been entered on the self-employment (full) pages (before tax adjustments).

The following items are included in the expenses shown in her accounts:

- Wages and salaries includes her drawings of £20,000
- Telephone costs include £400 for private calls
- Bank charges include £530 interest on her credit card which is for personal use
- Advertising includes entertaining customers costing £1,600, and a staff party costing £450

Deborah has also spent £29,000 on equipment in October 2016 and wishes to claim the maximum Annual Investment Allowance.

Required:

Complete, as far as possible, the remainder of pages 1 to 3 of the full self employment supplementary pages that follow. (The 2015/16 form has been used as the 2016/17 version was not available when this book was published.)

Note that these pages relate to the accounting period, not the basis period. (The details relating to the basis period would be dealt with on supplementary page 4, but are not assessable.)

HM Revenue & Customs

Self-employment (full)

Tax year 6 April 2015 to 5 April 2016 (2015-16)

Please read the 'Self-employment (full) notes' to check if you should use this page or the 'Self-employment (short)' page.

To get notes and helpsheets that will help you fill in this form, go to www.gov.uk/self-assessment-forms-and-helpsheets

Your name	Your Unique Taxpayer Reference (UTR)
Deborah Baker	

Business details

1 Business name – unless it is in your own name

2 Description of business

Trader

3 First line of your business address – unless you work from home

4 Postcode of your business address

5 If the details in boxes 1, 2, 3 or 4 have changed in the last 12 months, put 'X' in the box and give details in the 'Any other information' box

6 If your business started after 5 April 2015, enter the start date DD MM YYYY

0 1 1 0 2 0 1 6

7 If your business ceased after 5 April 2015 but before 6 April 2016, enter the final date of trading

8 Date your books or accounts start – the beginning of your accounting period

0 1 1 0 2 0 1 6

9 Date your books or accounts are made up to or the end of your accounting period – read the notes if you have filled in box 6 or 7

3 0 0 9 2 0 1 7

10 If you used the cash basis, money actually received and paid out, to calculate your income and expenses, put 'X' in the box – read the notes

Other information

11 If your accounting date has changed permanently, put 'X' in the box

12 If your accounting date has changed more than once since 2010, put 'X' in the box

13 If special arrangements apply, put 'X' in the box – read the notes

14 If you provided the information about your 2015–16 profit on last year's tax return, put 'X' in the box – read the notes

Business income

15 Your turnover – the takings, fees, sales or money earned by your business

£ 196000 . 0 0

16 Any other business income not included in box 15

£ . 0 0

Business expenses

Please read the 'Self-employment (full) notes' before filling in this section.

Total expenses

If your annual turnover was below £82,000, you may just put your total expenses in box 31

Disallowable expenses

Use this column if the figures in boxes 17 to 30 include disallowable amounts

17 Cost of goods bought for resale or goods used

£ 5 8 5 0 0 . 0 0

32

£ . 0 0

18 Construction industry – payments to subcontractors

£ . 0 0

33

£ . 0 0

19 Wages, salaries and other staff costs

£ 4 3 8 0 0 . 0 0

34

£ . 0 0

20 Car, van and travel expenses

£ . 0 0

35

£ . 0 0

21 Rent, rates, power and insurance costs

£ 9 8 6 0 . 0 0

36

£ . 0 0

22 Repairs and renewals of property and equipment

£ . 0 0

37

£ . 0 0

23 Phone, fax, stationery and other office costs

£ 2 1 0 0 . 0 0

38

£ . 0 0

24 Advertising and business entertainment costs

£ 3 0 4 0 . 0 0

39

£ . 0 0

25 Interest on bank and other loans

£ . 0 0

40

£ . 0 0

26 Bank, credit card and other financial charges

£ 1 5 0 0 . 0 0

41

£ . 0 0

27 Irrecoverable debts written off

£ . 0 0

42

£ . 0 0

28 Accountancy, legal and other professional fees

£ 2 0 0 0 . 0 0

43

£ . 0 0

29 Depreciation and loss/profit on sale of assets

£ 2 9 0 0 . 0 0

44

£ . 0 0

30 Other business expenses

£ . 0 0

45

£ . 0 0

31 Total expenses (total of boxes 17 to 30)

£ 1 2 3 7 0 0 . 0 0

46 Total disallowable expenses (total of boxes 32 to 45)

£ . 0 0

Net profit or loss

47 **Net profit** – if your business income is more than your expenses (if box 15 + box 16 minus box 31 is positive)

£ 7 2 3 0 0 . 0 0

48 **Or, net loss** – if your expenses are more than your business income (if box 31 minus (box 15 + box 16) is positive)

£ . 0 0

Tax allowances for vehicles and equipment (capital allowances)

There are 'capital' tax allowances for vehicles, equipment and certain buildings used in your business (don't include the cost of these in your business expenses). Please read the 'Self-employment (full) notes' and use the examples to work out your capital allowances.

49 **Annual Investment Allowance**

£ . 0 0

50 **Capital allowances at 18% on equipment, including cars with lower CO_2 emissions**

£ . 0 0

51 **Capital allowances at 8% on equipment, including cars with higher CO_2 emissions**

£ . 0 0

52 **Restricted capital allowances for cars costing more than £12,000** – if bought before 6 April 2009

£ . 0 0

Box 53 is not in use

54 **Business Premises Renovation Allowance (Assisted Areas only)** – read the notes

£ . 0 0

55 **100% and other enhanced capital allowances** – read the notes

£ . 0 0

56 **Allowances on sale or cessation of business use (where you have disposed of assets for less than their tax value)**

£ . 0 0

57 **Total capital allowances (total of boxes 49 to 56)**

£ . 0 0

58 **Balancing charge on sale or cessation of business use (only where Business Premises Renovation Allowance has been claimed)** – read the notes

£ . 0 0

59 **Balancing charge on sales of other assets or on the cessation of business use (where you have disposed of assets for more than their tax value)**

£ . 0 0

Calculating your taxable profit or loss

You may have to adjust your net profit or loss for disallowable expenses or capital allowances to arrive at your taxable profit or your loss for tax purposes. Please read the 'Self-employment (full) notes' and fill in the boxes below that apply.

60 **Goods and services for your own use** – read the notes

£ . 0 0

61 **Total additions to net profit or deductions from net loss (box 46 + box 58 + box 59 + box 60)**

£ . 0 0

62 **Income, receipts and other profits included in business income or expenses but not taxable as business profits**

£ . 0 0

63 **Total deductions from net profit or additions to net loss (box 57 + box 62)**

£ . 0 0

64 **Net business profit for tax purposes (if box 47 + box 61 minus (box 48 + box 63) is positive)**

£ . 0 0

65 **Net business loss for tax purposes (if box 48 + box 63 minus (box 47 + box 61) is positive)**

£ . 0 0

8 Capital gains tax for individuals

8.1 Select the appropriate procedure for a capital gains tax computation of an individual by ticking the appropriate column. Assume that there is no claim for gift relief where appropriate.

	Use Actual Proceeds	Use market value for proceeds	No gain or loss basis
Sale of asset for £5,000 to a friend. Market value of asset is £20,000			
Gift of asset to friend. Market value of asset is £20,000			
Sale of asset to business partner's wife for £5,000. Market value of asset is £20,000			
Gift of asset to civil partner. Market value of asset is £20,000			
Sale of asset to business partner's grandson for £5,000. Market value of asset is £20,000			
Sale of business asset to an unconnected limited company			
Sale of asset to husband for £20,000. Market value of asset is £5,000			

8.2 Adam purchased and sold shares in Beeco Limited as follows:

- 15 April 2005   Purchased 5,600 shares for £14,560
- 12 January 2017   Sold 1,400 shares for £4,060
- 1 February 2017   Purchased 2,800 shares for £6,160
- 31 March 2017   Sold 7,000 shares for £20,000

(a) The gain / loss on the sale of shares on 12 January 2017 is

£ _____

(b) The gain / loss on the sale of shares on 31 March 2017 is

£ _____

8.3   Poppy Price is a sole trader. She purchased a warehouse in October 2002 for £280,000, and sold it in April 2016 for £430,000. She purchased a shop in October 2016 for £390,000.

   (a)   Complete the following table relating to the gain on the sale of the warehouse, and any deferral of that gain. This was her only capital gain in 2016/17.

	£
Sale proceeds	
Cost	
Total gain	
Deferred gain	
Gain chargeable immediately	
Annual exempt amount	
Amount subject to CGT	

   (b)   The cost of the shop will be deemed to be £ [   ] when it is ultimately sold.

8.4   The following statements relate to entrepreneurs' relief. State whether each of the statements is true or false.

		True	False
(a)	It is subject to a lifetime limit of £10,000,000 per individual		
(b)	It works by charging the gain at 8%		
(c)	All disposals made by an individual are eligible		
(d)	It can relate to the disposal of shares held in a 'personal trading company'		
(e)	It is subject to a lifetime limit of £100,000,000		
(f)	It works by charging the gain at 10%		
(g)	It effectively uses up the basic rate band so other gains that are not eligible are more likely to be taxed at 20% or 28%		

8.5 There are similarities and differences between chargeable gains for companies subject to Corporation Tax, and Capital Gains Tax for individuals.

Select the rules and reliefs that apply to either or both companies and individuals by ticking the appropriate columns in the following table.

	Companies (Corporation Tax)	Individuals (Capital Gains Tax)
Gift relief		
Rollover relief		
Annual exempt amount		
Indexation allowance		
Chattel rules		
Entrepreneurs' relief		
Part disposal rules		

Answers to chapter activities

1 Introduction to business taxation

1.1   **(a)**, **(c)**, **(d)** and **(e)** are true; **(b)** is false.

1.2

	Period return relates to	Latest return submission date	Latest tax payment date
Corporation Tax	Chargeable accounting period	12 months after end of period that accounts are based on	9 months and one day after end of chargeable accounting period
Income Tax	Tax year	31 January following tax year	31 January following tax year

1.3   **(a)**   £34,940

    (b)   £3,184.60

1.4   **(a)**, **(b)**, **(c)** and **(d)** are true; **(e)** and **(f)** are false.

1.5   The final submission dates for tax returns are as follows:

    A sole trader with accounts made up to 31 March 2017: **31 January 2018**

    A sole trader with accounts made up to 30 June 2017: **31 January 2019**

    A limited company with accounts made up to 31 December 2016: **31 December 2017**

2 Corporation tax – trading profits

2.1

	Add to net profit	Deduct from net profit	No adjustment required
Depreciation	✔		
Discount received			✔
Directors' salaries			✔
Dividends received		✔	
Rent receivable		✔	
Rent payable			✔
Interest payable			✔
Advertising costs			✔
Entertaining customers	✔		

2.2 The adjusted trading profit (before capital allowances) is:

(c) £40,000 *Workings: (£37,000 – £12,000 + £13,000 + £2,000)*

2.3 **(a)**, **(d)** and **(g)** are true; **(b)**, **(c)**, **(e)** and **(f)** are false.

2.4 (e) The trading profits for the long period are adjusted for tax purposes (before capital allowances), and the result is time-apportioned into two chargeable accounting periods. Separate capital allowance computations are carried out for each chargeable accounting period, and then deducted from each of the adjusted trading profits

2.5 The maximum amount of loss that could be set against the taxable total profits for 2015 is

(a) £56,000 *(the loss must first be set against the £25,000 investment income and gains of 2016 before it can be carried back to the previous year)*

3 Corporation tax – capital allowances

3.1

	Qualify	Do not qualify
Car for employee's private use	✔	
Office furniture	✔	
Capital expenditure on software	✔	
Payments for vehicle on operating lease		✔
Vehicles bought on credit	✔	
Buildings		✔
Equipment bought through hire purchase	✔	

3.2 The AIA that can be claimed is **£60,000**

The first year allowance that can be claimed at 100% is **£26,000**

The writing down allowance that can be claimed at 18% is **£0**

The writing down allowance that can be claimed at 8% is **£1,760**

The total capital allowance that can be claimed is **£87,760**

3.3

	AIA (to limit)	Main pool	Special rate pool	100% FYA
Car emissions of 185 g/km			✔	
Car emissions of 99 g/km		✔		
Machinery	✔			
Zero-emission goods vehicle				✔
Car emissions of 125 g/km		✔		
Water-efficient plant				✔

3.4   **(b)** and **(d)** are true; **(a)**, **(c)** and **(e)** are false.

3.5   **Capital Allowance Computation**

	Main pool	Special rate pool	Capital allowances
	£	£	£
WDV bf	120,000	19,000	
add			
Acquisitions			
without FYA or AIA:			
Car (190 g/km)		35,000	
Acquisitions			
qualifying for AIA			
Machinery £60,000			
AIA £(60,000)			60,000
Excess -	0		
less			
Proceeds of disposals:	(5,000)	(7,000)	
	115,000	47,000	
18% WDA	(20,700)		20,700
8% WDA		(3,760)	3,760
WDV cf	94,300	43,240	
Total Capital Allowances			84,460

4 Corporation tax – chargeable gains

4.1

	Actual proceeds	Market value	£6,000	Zero
Sale of asset for £15,000 to Director who owns 80% of shares in company. Market value of asset is £35,000		✔		
Gift of asset to unconnected individual (non-shareholder)		✔		
Sale of asset to company employee (non-shareholder) at below market value	✔			
Sale of chattel for £4,000 (its market value) that had originally cost £10,000			✔	
Destruction of an uninsured asset during fire				✔
Sale of asset for £15,000 to Director who owns 10% of shares in company. Market value of asset is £35,000	✔			
Shares owned in an unconnected company that have become worthless due to the company's liquidation				✔

4.2   Proceeds: £10,000

Cost: £3,500

Indexation allowance: £1,866

Gain: £4,634

Chattel restriction on gain: £6,667

The chattel restriction will NOT have any effect on the original gain.

4.3

	No. Shares	Cost £	Indexed cost £
Purchase	8,000	19,500	19,500
Index to July 2003			2,223
Rights issue	200	360	360
Sub total	8,200	19,860	22,083
Index to April 2016			9,761
Sub total	8,200	19,860	31,844
Disposal	(6,000)	(14,532)	(23,300)
Pool balance	2,200	5,328	8,544

Proceeds	£24,000
Indexed Cost	£23,300
Gain	£700

4.4   Proceeds: £40,000

Cost[1]: £36,000

Indexation allowance: £19,188

Gain or (Loss)[2]: £0

Notes:

(1)   Cost is calculated as £90,000 x £40,000 / (£40,000 + £60,000)

(2)   Indexation cannot create a loss

4.5   Proceeds[1]: £6,000

Cost: £7,500

Indexation allowance[2]: £0

Gain or (Loss): (£1,500)

Notes:

(1)   Deemed proceeds are £6,000 for a chattel sold at a loss for under £6,000

(2)   Indexation allowance cannot be used to increase a loss

5 Corporation tax – calculating the tax

5.1

Loss	Rules that can apply
Trading Loss	(e)
Capital Loss	(f)
Rental Loss	(a)

5.2

Tax calculation
Turnover

145 Total turnover from trade £ [_____] · 0 0

150 Banks, building societies, insurance companies and other financial concerns –
put an 'X' in this box if you do not have a recognised turnover and have not made an entry in box 145 [ ]

Income

155 Trading profits £ [1 3 5 0 0 0 0] · 0 0

160 Trading losses brought forward claimed against profits £ [1 3 0 0 0 0] · 0 0

165 Net trading profits – *box 155 minus box 160* £ [1 2 2 0 0 0 0] · 0 0

170 Bank, building society or other interest, and profits
from non-trading loan relationships £ [_____] · 0 0

172 Put an 'X' in box 172 if the figure in box 170 is net of
carrying back a deficit from a later accounting period [ ]

175 Annual payments not otherwise charged to Corporation Tax
and from which Income Tax has not been deducted £ [_____] · 0 0

Income *continued*

180 Non-exempt dividends or distributions from
non–UK resident companies   £ ⬚⬚⬚⬚⬚⬚⬚⬚⬚⬚⬚ · 0 0

185 Income from which Income Tax has been deducted   £ ⬚⬚⬚⬚⬚⬚⬚⬚⬚⬚⬚ · 0 0

190 Income from a property business   £ ⬚⬚⬚⬚ 2 5 0 0 0 0 · 0 0

195 Non-trading gains on intangible fixed assets   £ ⬚⬚⬚⬚⬚⬚⬚⬚⬚⬚⬚ · 0 0

200 Tonnage Tax profits   £ ⬚⬚⬚⬚⬚⬚⬚⬚⬚⬚⬚ · 0 0

205 Income not falling under any other heading   £ ⬚⬚⬚⬚⬚⬚⬚⬚⬚⬚⬚ · 0 0

Chargeable gains

210 Gross chargeable gains   £ ⬚⬚⬚⬚ 2 2 0 0 0 0 · 0 0

215 Allowable losses including losses brought forward   £ ⬚⬚⬚⬚ 2 2 0 0 0 0 · 0 0

220 Net chargeable gains *- box 210 minus box 215*   £ ⬚⬚⬚⬚ 1 7 0 0 0 0 · 0 0

Profits before deductions and reliefs

225 Losses brought forward against certain investment income   £ ⬚⬚⬚⬚⬚⬚⬚⬚⬚⬚⬚ · 0 0

230 Non-trade deficits on loan relationships (including interest)
and derivative contracts (financial instruments)
brought forward   £ ⬚⬚⬚⬚⬚⬚⬚⬚⬚⬚⬚ · 0 0

235 Profits before other deductions and reliefs – *net sum of
boxes 165 to 205 and 220 minus sum of boxes 225 and 230*   £ ⬚⬚⬚⬚ 1 6 4 0 0 0 0 · 0 0

5.3   **(b)**, **(c)**, **(e)**, **(f)** and **(g)** are true; **(a)** and **(d)** are false.

6 Income tax – trading profits

6.1

	Badges of Trade
Reason for acquisition and sale of item(s)	✔
Whether individual enjoys carrying out the activity	
Whether there is a profit motive	✔
How long the individual has owned the item(s) before sale	✔
Whether the individual only sells via computer sites	
Whether any supplementary work is carried out on the item(s) before sale	✔
Whether the individual considers the activity to be his hobby	
How often the individual carries out similar transactions	✔
Whether the items bought and sold (the subject matter) are used personally by the individual before sale	✔

6.2

	Allowable expenditure	Non-allowable expenditure
Cost of sales	✔	
Entertaining staff	✔	
Fines for lawbreaking by business owner		✔
Gifts of food or drink to customers		✔
Trade bad debts written off	✔	
Salary and NIC of business owner		✔
Depreciation		✔
Loss on sale of non-current assets		✔

6.3

	£	£
Net Profit		112,310
Add		
Goods for own use	2,000	
Depreciation	22,020	
Laura's salary	45,000	
Laura's son's salary (unreasonable)	28,000	
Gifts of bottles of wine	2,400	
Laura's son's car expenses	3,800	
Increase in general bad debt provision	2,600	
		105,820
		218,130
Less		
Capital allowances		10,400
Adjusted trading profits		207,730

6.4   The AIA that can be claimed is **£44,400**[(1)]

The single asset pool writing down allowance that can be claimed is **£2,160**[(2)]

The special rate pool writing down allowance that can be claimed is **£0**

The total capital allowance that can be claimed is **£46,560**[(3)]

The total written down value carried forward is **£16,400**[(4)]

Workings:

(1)   *£30,000 + (£18,000 x 80%) = £44,400 (below AIA limit for this period.)*

(2)   *£20,000 x 18% x 60% = £2,160*

(3)   *£44,400 + £2,160 = £46,560*

(4)   *£20,000 – (£20,000 x 18%) = £16,400*

6.5   (b)   £37,000

The rules for a sole trader or partnership mean that the loss can be set off against the previous year's total income without first setting off in the current year.

7 Income tax – further issues

7.1 **(a)** The tax year in which he started trading was **2014/15**.

(b) His taxable profits in his first tax year of trading were **£43,000**.

(c) His taxable profits in his second tax year of trading were **£108,000**.

(d) His taxable profits in his third tax year of trading were **£92,000**.

(e) His overlap profits were **£27,000**.

(f) His overlap profits are deducted from the profits in the final year of trading, or on a change of accounting date

7.2 **(d)** 6 April 2015 to 5 April 2016

7.3 **(1)**

	Total	Pete	Heather	Ash
	£	£	£	£
1 Jan - 31 August 2016	80,000	40,000	40,000	0
1 Sept - 31 Dec 2016	40,000	15,000	15,000	10,000
Total	120,000	55,000	55,000	10,000

(2) **(c)** 1/9/2016 - 5/4/2017

7.4

		£
Payment on 31 January 2017	Balance of tax and NIC for 2015/16	3,600
	Payment on account for 2016/17	5,800
	Total	9,400
Payment on 31 July 2017	Payment on account for 2016/17	5,800

7.5

HM Revenue & Customs

Self-employment (full)

Tax year 6 April 2015 to 5 April 2016 (2015-16)

Please read the 'Self-employment (full) notes' to check if you should use this page or the 'Self-employment (short)' page.

To get notes and helpsheets that will help you fill in this form, go to **www.gov.uk/self-assessment-forms-and-helpsheets**

Your name

D e b o r a h   B a k e r

Your Unique Taxpayer Reference (UTR)

Business details

1 Business name – unless it is in your own name

2 Description of business

T r a d e r

3 First line of your business address – unless you work from home

4 Postcode of your business address

5 If the details in boxes 1, 2, 3 or 4 have changed in the last 12 months, put 'X' in the box and give details in the 'Any other information' box

6 If your business started after 5 April 2015, enter the start date DD MM YYYY

0 1 1 0 2 0 1 6

7 If your business ceased after 5 April 2015 but before 6 April 2016, enter the final date of trading

8 Date your books or accounts start – the beginning of your accounting period

0 1 1 0 2 0 1 6

9 Date your books or accounts are made up to or the end of your accounting period – read the notes if you have filled in box 6 or 7

3 0 0 9 2 0 1 7

10 If you used the cash basis, money actually received and paid out, to calculate your income and expenses, put 'X' in the box – read the notes

Other information

11 If your accounting date has changed permanently, put 'X' in the box

12 If your accounting date has changed more than once since 2010, put 'X' in the box

13 If special arrangements apply, put 'X' in the box – read the notes

14 If you provided the information about your 2015-16 profit on last year's tax return, put 'X' in the box – read the notes

Business income

15 Your turnover – the takings, fees, sales or money earned by your business

£   1 9 6 0 0 0 . 0 0

16 Any other business income not included in box 15

£ . 0 0

SA103F 2016   Page SEF 1   HMRC 12/15

Business expenses

Please read the 'Self-employment (full) notes' before filling in this section.

Total expenses

If your annual turnover was below £82,000, you may just put your total expenses in box 31

Disallowable expenses

Use this column if the figures in boxes 17 to 30 include disallowable amounts

17 Cost of goods bought for resale or goods used

£ 5 8 5 0 0 · 0 0

32 £ · 0 0

18 Construction industry – payments to subcontractors

£ · 0 0

33 £ · 0 0

19 Wages, salaries and other staff costs

£ 4 3 8 0 0 · 0 0

34 £ 2 0 0 0 0 · 0 0

20 Car, van and travel expenses

£ · 0 0

35 £ · 0 0

21 Rent, rates, power and insurance costs

£ 9 8 6 0 · 0 0

36 £ · 0 0

22 Repairs and renewals of property and equipment

£ · 0 0

37 £ · 0 0

23 Phone, fax, stationery and other office costs

£ 2 1 0 0 · 0 0

38 £ 4 0 0 · 0 0

24 Advertising and business entertainment costs

£ 3 0 4 0 · 0 0

39 £ 1 6 0 0 · 0 0

25 Interest on bank and other loans

£ · 0 0

40 £ · 0 0

26 Bank, credit card and other financial charges

£ 1 5 0 0 · 0 0

41 £ 5 3 0 · 0 0

27 Irrecoverable debts written off

£ · 0 0

42 £ · 0 0

28 Accountancy, legal and other professional fees

£ 2 0 0 0 · 0 0

43 £ · 0 0

29 Depreciation and loss/profit on sale of assets

£ 2 9 0 0 · 0 0

44 £ 2 9 0 0 · 0 0

30 Other business expenses

£ · 0 0

45 £ · 0 0

31 Total expenses (total of boxes 17 to 30)

£ 1 2 3 7 0 0 · 0 0

46 Total disallowable expenses (total of boxes 32 to 45)

£ 2 5 4 3 0 · 0 0

Net profit or loss

47 **Net profit** – if your business income is more than your expenses (if box 15 + box 16 minus box 31 is positive)

£ 7 2 3 0 0 . 0 0

48 **Or, net loss** – if your expenses are more than your business income (if box 31 minus (box 15 + box 16) is positive)

£ . 0 0

Tax allowances for vehicles and equipment (capital allowances)

There are 'capital' tax allowances for vehicles, equipment and certain buildings used in your business (don't include the cost of these in your business expenses). Please read the 'Self-employment (full) notes' and use the examples to work out your capital allowances.

49 **Annual Investment Allowance**

£ 2 9 0 0 0 . 0 0

50 **Capital allowances at 18% on equipment, including cars with lower CO$_2$ emissions**

£ . 0 0

51 **Capital allowances at 8% on equipment, including cars with higher CO$_2$ emissions**

£ . 0 0

52 **Restricted capital allowances for cars costing more than £12,000** – if bought before 6 April 2009

£ . 0 0

Box 53 is not in use

54 **Business Premises Renovation Allowance (Assisted Areas only)** – read the notes

£ . 0 0

55 **100% and other enhanced capital allowances** – read the notes

£ . 0 0

56 **Allowances on sale or cessation of business use (where you have disposed of assets for less than their tax value)**

£ . 0 0

57 **Total capital allowances (total of boxes 49 to 56)**

£ 2 9 0 0 0 . 0 0

58 **Balancing charge on sale or cessation of business use (only where Business Premises Renovation Allowance has been claimed)** – read the notes

£ . 0 0

59 **Balancing charge on sales of other assets or on the cessation of business use (where you have disposed of assets for more than their tax value)**

£ . 0 0

Calculating your taxable profit or loss

You may have to adjust your net profit or loss for disallowable expenses or capital allowances to arrive at your taxable profit or your loss for tax purposes. Please read the 'Self-employment (full) notes' and fill in the boxes below that apply.

60 **Goods and services for your own use** – read the notes

£ . 0 0

61 **Total additions to net profit or deductions from net loss (box 46 + box 58 + box 59 + box 60)**

£ 2 5 4 3 0 . 0 0

62 **Income, receipts and other profits included in business income or expenses but not taxable as business profits**

£ . 0 0

63 **Total deductions from net profit or additions to net loss (box 57 + box 62)**

£ 2 9 0 0 0 . 0 0

64 **Net business profit for tax purposes (if box 47 + box 61 minus (box 48 + box 63) is positive)**

£ 6 8 7 3 0 . 0 0

65 **Net business loss for tax purposes (if box 48 + box 63 minus (box 47 + box 61) is positive)**

£ . 0 0

8 Capital gains tax for individuals

8.1

	Use Actual Proceeds	Use market value for proceeds	No gain or loss basis
Sale of asset for £5,000 to a friend. Market value of asset is £20,000	✔		
Gift of asset to friend. Market value of asset is £20,000		✔	
Sale of asset to business partner's wife for £5,000. Market value of asset is £20,000		✔	
Gift of asset to civil partner. Market value of asset is £20,000			✔
Sale of asset to business partner's grandson for £5,000. Market value of asset is £20,000		✔	
Sale of business asset to an unconnected limited company	✔		
Sale of asset to husband for £20,000. Market value of asset is £5,000			✔

8.2 **(a)** The **gain** on the sale of shares on 12 January 2017 is **£980**.

The shares sold on 12 January are matched with 1,400 of those bought on 1 February (within the following 30 days), leaving 1,400 of that purchase unmatched.

(b) The **gain** on the sale of shares on 31 March 2017 is **£2,360**.

The shares sold on 31 March are matched with the pooled purchases of 5,600 + 1,400 (balance) = 7,000 shares, costing a total of £17,640.

8.3   **(a)**

	£
Sale proceeds	430,000
Cost	280,000
Total gain	150,000
Deferred gain	110,000
Gain chargeable immediately	40,000
Annual exempt amount	11,100
Amount subject to CGT	28,900

(b)   The cost of the shop will be deemed to be **£280,000** when it is ultimately sold.

Workings: (£390,000 – £110,000).

8.4   **(a)**, **(d)**, **(f)** and **(g)** are true; **(b)**, **(c)** and **(e)** are false.

8.5

	Companies (Corporation Tax)	Individuals (Capital Gains Tax)
Gift relief		✔
Rollover relief	✔	✔
Annual exempt amount		✔
Indexation allowance	✔	
Chattel rules	✔	✔
Entrepreneurs' relief		✔
Part disposal rules	✔	✔

Practice assessment 1

Task 1

(a) From the following list, select the correct treatment of each item when computing taxable trading profits, by ticking the appropriate column.

	Disallow and add back	Disallow and deduct	Allow (no action)
(a) Discount received			
(b) Loss on sale of non-current asset			
(c) Gifts of chocolates (with logo) costing £20 each to customers			
(d) Rental income			
(e) Installation of new production machinery			
(f) Advertising expenditure			

(b) Julie started trading on 1 December 2014, making her first set of accounts up to 30 April 2016. Her adjusted trading profits were:

Period ended 30 April 2016   £54,400

Year ended 30 April 2017   £42,000

Complete the following table to show the basis period, and profits for the second and third tax years. Also show the total overlap profits.

Tax year (YYYY/YY)	Basis period start date (DD/MM/YY)	Basis period end date (DD/MM/YY)	Profits £	Total overlap profits £

Task 2

Molly and Nigel are in partnership, trading as carpet fitters, with an accounting year end of 31 March. They had shared profits 3:2 for some time. On 1 November 2016 their arrangements changed to the rates shown below.

	Molly	**Nigel**
Salary per year	£12,000	£18,000
Partners' capital	£48,000	£18,000
Interest on capital	4% pa	4% pa
Profit sharing percentage	55%	45%

The taxable profit of the partnership for the year ended 31 March 2017 was £109,920.

(a) Show the division of the profits between the partners for the year ended 31 March 2017 using the table below. Round answers to the nearest £ if appropriate.

To 31 October 2016	Molly £	Nigel £
Share of profits		
From 1 November 2016	**Molly £**	**Nigel £**
Interest on capital		
Salary		
Share of profits		

(b) Calculate Molly's National Insurance Contributions for 2016/17. Round answers to the nearest penny.

	£
Class 2 NIC	
Class 4 NIC at 9%	
Class 4 NIC at 2%	

Task 3

A company has the following information regarding its non-current assets for a 12-month CAP, ending on 30/6/2016.

	£
Written down values brought forward:	
General (main) pool	105,000
Special rate pool	17,000
Additions:	
Computer System (bought January 2016)	290,000
New car for Sales Director (emissions 44 g/km)	25,000
Disposals:	
Machinery	5,000

Calculate the maximum capital allowances for the CAP.

Task 4

Alison Amsterdam and Bob Bolton have been trading in partnership for many years with accounting year ends of 31 March. They trade in wholesale fabric. The trade profits and interest received are both divided between the partners in the ratio 3:2.

In the accounting year ended 31/3/2017, the partnership had trade profits of £80,000 and received interest of £1,600.

Complete page 6 of the partnership tax return (the 2015/16 version is reproduced on the opposite page) relating to:

· the whole partnership, and

· Alison Amsterdam's share of profits and interest

PARTNERSHIP STATEMENT (SHORT) for the year ended 5 April 2016

Please read these instructions before completing the Statement

Use these pages to allocate partnership income if the only income for the relevant return period was trading and professional income or taxed interest and alternative finance receipts from banks and building societies. Otherwise you must download or ask the SA Orderline for the 'Partnership Statement (Full)' pages to record details of the allocation of all the partnership income. Go to www.gov.uk/self-assessment-forms-and-helpsheets

Step 1   Fill in boxes 1 to 29 and boxes A and B as appropriate. Get the figures you need from the relevant boxes in the Partnership Tax Return. Complete a separate Statement for each accounting period covered by this Partnership Tax Return and for each trade or profession carried on by the partnership.

Step 2   Then allocate the amounts in boxes 11 to 29 attributable to each partner using the allocation columns on this page and page 7, read the Partnership Tax Return Guide, go to www.gov.uk/self-assessment-forms-and-helpsheets
If the partnership has more than 3 partners, please photocopy page 7.

Step 3   Each partner will need a copy of their allocation of income to fill in their personal tax return.

PARTNERSHIP INFORMATION
If the partnership business includes a trade or profession, enter here the accounting period for which appropriate items in this statement are returned.

Start   **1**   /   /

End   **2**   /   /

Nature of trade   **3**

MIXED PARTNERSHIPS

Tick here if this Statement is drawn up using Corporation Tax rules   **4**

Tick here if this Statement is drawn up using tax rules for non-residents   **5**

Individual partner details

6   Name of partner

Address

Postcode

Date appointed as a partner (if during 2014–15 or 2015–16)

7   /   /

Date ceased to be a partner (if during 2014–15 or 2015–16)

9   /   /

Partner's Unique Taxpayer Reference (UTR)

8

Partner's National Insurance number

10

Partnership's profits, losses, income, tax credits, etc

Tick this box if the items entered in the box had foreign tax taken off

Partner's share of profits, losses, income, tax credits, etc

Copy figures in boxes 11 to 29 to boxes in the individual's **Partnership (short)** pages as shown below

* **for an accounting period ended in 2015–16 ▼**

from box 3.83	Profit from a trade or profession	**A** **11** £	Profit **11** £	Copy this figure to box 8
from box 3.82	Adjustment on change of basis	**11A** £	**11A** £	Copy this figure to box 10
from box 3.84	Loss from a trade or profession	**B** **12** £	Loss **12** £	Copy this figure to box 8
from box 10.4	Business Premises Renovation Allowance	**12A** £	**12A** £	Copy this figure to box 15

* **for the period 6 April 2015 to 5 April 2016***

from box 7.9A	UK taxed interest and taxed alternative finance receipts	**22** £	**22** £	Copy this figure to box 28
from box 3.97	CIS deductions made by contractors on account of tax	**24** £	**24** £	Copy this figure to box 30
from box 3.98	Other tax taken off trading income	**24A** £	**24A** £	Copy this figure to box 31
from box 7.8A	Income Tax taken off	**25** £	**25** £	Copy this figure to box 29
from box 3.117	Partnership charges	**29** £	**29** £	Copy this figure to box 4, 'Other tax reliefs' section on page Ai 2 in your personal tax return

* if you are a 'CT Partnership' see the Partnership Tax Return Guide

Task 5

(a) Delta Limited has produced the following results for the 16-month accounting period to 31 December 2016.

Trading Profits for 16-month period (before capital allowances)	£800,000
Capital Allowances: y/e 31/8/2016	£54,000
4 months to 31/12/2016	£19,000
Chargeable Gains: Disposal 12/12/2015	£36,000
Disposal 19/4/2016	£14,000
Disposal 10/10/2016	£41,000
Rental Income – monthly amount	£2,000
Gift Aid Payment (paid 31/12/2016)	£6,000

Use the following table to calculate the TTP for each CAP.

	CAP 12 months to 31/8/2016 £	CAP 4 months to 31/12/2016 £
Trading Profits before CAs		
Capital Allowances		
Trading Profits		
Chargeable Gains		
Rental Income		
Sub total		
Gift Aid		
TTP		

(b) Calculate the Corporation Tax payable by Delta Limited for the two accounting periods.

	CAP 12 months to 31/8/2016 £	CAP 4 months to 31/12/2016 £
Corporation Tax Payable		

Task 6

(a) Sue has been trading for many years, and her Income Tax and NIC liability is as follows:

2013/14	£15,600
2014/15	£18,100
2015/16	£19,300

Complete the following table to show the details and amounts that Sue will pay in the calendar year 2017.

Tax year (YYYY/YY)	Payment date (DD/MM/YYYY)	Payment on account / Balancing payment	Amount £

(b) National Limited has an accounting year end of 31 August 2016. The final date for payment of Corporation Tax for this CAP is:

Task 7

(a) Identify whether each of the following statements is true or false.

		True	False
(a)	Interest is payable by self-employed individuals on late balancing payments and underpayments of amounts due on account		
(b)	A £100 late submission penalty is payable for self-employed individuals only if their tax return is late by more than 60 days		
(c)	A 'reasonable excuse' by an individual for a late return may be sufficient to prevent a penalty if HMRC consider it to be valid		
(d)	If a taxpayer took reasonable care, yet the return still contained an error, there will be no penalty		
(e)	A sole trader who starts trading must notify HMRC within six months of the end of tax year		
(f)	If HMRC complete an enquiry into a company and submit a closure notice, the company has 30 days to appeal the decision		

(b) Marmalade Limited made an unprompted disclosure of an error which was considered to be due to lack of reasonable care. The additional Corporation Tax payable as a result was £1,500. The penalty will be as follows:

Minimum £	
Maximum £	

Task 8

(a)   The following statements relate to how the trading losses of a limited company can be utilised. Identify whether each statement is true or false.

		True	False
(a)	When a trading loss is set against the taxable total profits of the period in which the loss arose this is carried out in priority to relief on any gift aid payments		
(b)	A trading loss can be carried forward against future profits from the same trade, but only for a maximum of two chargeable accounting periods		
(c)	A company trading loss can be carried back to the chargeable accounting period in the 12 months before the loss was incurred, regardless of whether it was first offset against the current CAP taxable total profits		
(d)	A trading loss can be carried forward to set against taxable total profits without time limit		
(e)	If a company changes its trade then it will be unable to offset previous losses from the original trade against profits from the new trade		
(f)	The trading income assessment for the chargeable accounting period in which a trading loss occurs will always be zero		
(g)	A small or medium sized company that has qualifying research and development expenditure and incurs a loss may choose to receive tax credits subject to limits		

Task 9

It is May 2017. A new client, David, has come to you to ask advice. David is a Director of a limited company that started trading on 1 January 2015. HMRC were notified that trading had started, but no other contact has been made with HMRC regarding Corporation Tax.

Accounts have been prepared for the year ended 31 December 2015 and it has been calculated that the Corporation Tax for that period will be £45,000. Unfortunately, since the accounts were prepared many of the sales and purchase invoices for the period were accidentally shredded.

Write a note that explains what deadlines have been missed and what penalties and / or interest the company could be liable for based on the above information.

Task 10

(a)   Analyse the following assets into those that are chargeable regarding CGT and those that are exempt.

	Chargeable	Exempt
Government Stocks (gilts)		
Shares in Limited Companies		
Trading Inventory		
Land		

(b)   Trolley Ltd sold an antique painting for £7,100 in April 2016. This was bought for £4,000 in August 2000. The indexation factor from August 2000 to April 2016 was 0.533.

Complete the following computation:

Proceeds: £ ☐

Cost: £ ☐

Indexation allowance: £ ☐

Gain: £ ☐

Chattel restriction on gain: £ ☐

State whether the chattel restriction will have any effect on the original gain.   YES / NO

Task 11

(a)   Perfect Ltd bought 9,000 shares in Toronto Ltd for £27,900 in October 2001. Bonus shares were issued in April 2002 at 1 for 10. Purchases of 5,000 shares were made in July 2003 for £3.80 per share. In April 2016, Perfect Ltd sold 10,000 of the shares for £5.00 per share.

Indexation factors were:

October 2001 to July 2003:   0.114

July 2003 to April 2016:   0.442

Calculate the pool balances remaining and the gain made on the share disposal.

	No. Shares	Cost £	Indexed Cost £

Proceeds	£
Indexed Cost	£
Gain	£

(b)   Carol purchased and sold shares in Ceeco Limited as follows:

10 April 2002	Purchased 5,000 shares for £15,000
12 January 2017	Sold 1,800 shares for £4,000
1 February 2017	Purchased 6,800 shares for £21,080
31 March 2017	Sold 10,000 shares for £40,000

(1)   The ⬚ gain / loss ⬚ on the sale of shares on 12 January 2017 is

£ ⬚

(2)   The ⬚ gain / loss ⬚ on the sale of shares on 31 March 2017 is

£ ⬚

Practice assessment 2

Task 1

Lisa has the following income statement:

	£	£
Gross profit		1,450,395
Wages and salaries	731,200	
Accountancy and legal costs	21,450	
Motor expenses	65,480	
Repairs and renewals	55,550	
Office expenses	42,690	
Depreciation	155,310	
Other expenses	41,840	1,113,520
Profit		336,875

Notes include:

Gross profit is after deducting bulk discounts given of	£15,300

Wages and salaries include:

Lisa's salary and personal pension contributions	£75,400
Lisa's son's salary (he works part-time in the office)	£7,400

Accountancy and legal costs comprise:

Legal fees to purchase new office building	£10,250
Annual accountancy and audit fee	£11,200

Motor expenses include:

Operating lease of 180 g/km car used for business by works manager	£11,660
Expenses of Lisa's car which is used 70% for the business	£12,500

Repairs and renewals include:

Repainting exterior of factory building	£40,000

Capital allowances have been calculated as	£21,380

(a)   Complete the following computation. You may not need to use all the lines provided.

	£
Profit	336,875
Disallowed items added back:	
Allowed items deducted:	
Adjusted trading profits	

(b)   Complete the following table by selecting the correct treatment of each item in the accounts of a sole trader when adjusting for tax purposes.

	Add back to profit	Deduct from profit	No adjustment required
(a) Loss on sale of non-current assets			
(b) Installation costs of new machinery			
(c) Discounts received for prompt payment			
(d) Interest received on deposit account			

(c) Josie has been trading for many years, making her accounts up to 30 June. In 2016/17 she changed her accounting date to 30 April, and produced accounts for the period 1 July 2016 to 30 April 2017. Her adjusted trading profits were:

Year ended 30 June 2015	£55,920
Year ended 30 June 2016	£49,800
Period ended 30 April 2017	£44,400

Josie had overlap profit brought forward from when she started the business of £3,000.

Complete the following table to show the basis periods, and profits for the tax years shown. Also show the total overlap profits to be carried forward.

Tax year	Basis period start date (DD/MM/YY)	Basis period end date (DD/MM/YY)	Profits £	Total overlap profits £
2016/17				
2017/18				

Task 2

Olly and Pete are in partnership, working as plasterers, with an accounting year end of 31 March. They had shared profits equally for some time. On 1 September 2016 their arrangements changed as shown below.

	Olly	Pete
Salary per year	£15,000	£12,000
Partners' capital	£30,000	£24,000
Interest on capital	5% pa	5% pa
Profit sharing percentage	40%	60%

The taxable profit of the partnership for the year ended 31 March 2017 was £92,160.

(a)   Show the division of the profits between the partners for the year ended 31 March 2017 using the table below. Round answers to the nearest £ if appropriate.

To 31 August 2016	Olly £	Pete £
Share of profits		
From 1 September 2016	**Olly £**	**Pete £**
Interest on capital		
Salary		
Share of profits		

(b)   The partnership agreement of Brian and Colin stipulates that Brian is entitled to 55% of partnership profits and Colin 45%.

The total partnership profits for 2016/17 were £89,600.

Complete the following table and calculate the Class 4 National Insurance Contributions for both Brian and Colin for 2016/17. Calculations should be carried out to the nearest penny.

	Profits	Class 4 at 9%	Class 4 at 2%	Total Class 4 NIC
	£	£	£	£
Brian				
Colin				

Task 3

Tintagel Limited had the following non-current asset information for the seven month period ending on 31 December 2016.

Balances brought forward on 1 June 2016:

General pool	£157,500
Special rate pool	£31,680

Additions during period:

Machinery	£139,334
Car (CO_2 emissions 61 g/km)	£29,500

The company was forced to cease trading on 30 April 2017, following an irrecoverable debt from a major customer.

The proceeds of the non-current assets that were sold on that date were:

Car purchased in previous CAP	£19,800
General pool machinery	£55,500
Special rate pool items	£22,100

Calculate the capital allowances for the CAP ended 31 December 2016, and the final CAP ended 30 April 2017.

Task 4

The following information relates to the chargeable accounting period 12 months to 31 January 2017 for Geebee Limited.

	£
Turnover	4,150,300
Trading profits	1,130,450
Trading losses brought forward	359,500
Net rental income	445,630
Chargeable gains	85,695
Capital losses brought forward	115,480

Complete the relevant boxes in the following extract from the CT600 Corporation Tax return for the company.

Tax calculation
Turnover

145 **Total turnover from trade**   £ [   ] . 0 0

150 **Banks, building societies, insurance companies and other financial concerns –**
put an 'X' in this box if you do not have a recognised turnover and have not made an entry in box 145   [ ]

Income

155 **Trading profits**   £ [   ] . 0 0

160 **Trading losses brought forward claimed against profits**   £ [   ] . 0 0

165 **Net trading profits** – *box 155 minus box 160*   £ [   ] . 0 0

170 **Bank, building society or other interest, and profits from non-trading loan relationships**   £ [   ] . 0 0

172 Put an 'X' in box 172 if the figure in box 170 is net of carrying back a deficit from a later accounting period   [ ]

175 **Annual payments not otherwise charged to Corporation Tax and from which Income Tax has not been deducted**   £ [   ] . 0 0

Income *continued*

180 Non-exempt dividends or distributions from non–UK resident companies   £ [ ] • 0 0

185 Income from which Income Tax has been deducted   £ [ ] • 0 0

190 Income from a property business   £ [ ] • 0 0

195 Non-trading gains on intangible fixed assets   £ [ ] • 0 0

200 Tonnage Tax profits   £ [ ] • 0 0

205 Income not falling under any other heading   £ [ ] • 0 0

Chargeable gains

210 Gross chargeable gains   £ [ ] • 0 0

215 Allowable losses including losses brought forward   £ [ ] • 0 0

220 Net chargeable gains - *box 210 minus box 215*   £ [ ] • 0 0

Profits before deductions and reliefs

225 Losses brought forward against certain investment income   £ [ ] • 0 0

230 Non-trade deficits on loan relationships (including interest) and derivative contracts (financial instruments) brought forward   £ [ ] • 0 0

235 Profits before other deductions and reliefs – *net sum of boxes 165 to 205 and 220 minus sum of boxes 225 and 230*   £ [ ] • 0 0

Task 5

(a)   Team Limited made up accounts for the 17 month period to 28 February 2017. The following details have been extracted for the period:

The company made a capital loss of £14,150 in September 2016, and capital gains of £19,660 in July 2016 and £19,475 in December 2016. The adjusted trading profits for the period were £160,871.

State the amounts to be taken into account in each of the following periods.

	First accounting period £	Second accounting period £
Capital gains		
Trading profits		

(b)   Calculate the Corporation Tax payable by Team Limited for the two accounting periods.

	CAP 12 months to 30/9/2016 £	CAP 5 months to 28/2/2017 £
Corporation Tax Payable		

Task 6

(a) Adam has been trading for many years, and his Income Tax and NIC liability is as follows:

2013/14   £9,600

2014/15   £15,450

2015/16   £13,500

Adam has not made any claim to reduce payments on account.

Complete the following table to show the total amounts that Adam will pay on the dates shown.

Payment date	Amount £
31 July 2016	
31 January 2017	
31 July 2017	

(b) Chef Limited has an accounting year end of 31 July 2016. The final date for payment of Corporation Tax for this CAP is:

Task 7

(a) Identify whether each of the following statements is true or false.

		True	False
(a)	Interest is payable by self-employed individuals on late balancing payments, but not on underpayments of amounts due on account		
(b)	A total late submission penalty is payable for self-employed individuals of £100, plus £10 per day if their tax return is late by between three and six months		
(c)	Online and paper-based returns have the same submission deadlines for individuals		
(d)	If a taxpayer took reasonable care, yet the return still contained an error, there can be a penalty		
(e)	A sole trader who fails to keep adequate records for the correct length of time can face a penalty of £3,000 per tax year		
(f)	Companies must submit a tax return online for each chargeable accounting period		

(b) Carrington Limited made a prompted disclosure of an error which was considered to be due to lack of reasonable care. The additional Corporation Tax payable as a result was £4,500. The penalty will be as follows:

Minimum £	
Maximum £	

Task 8

Tulip Limited has the following results from the last two years.

Year ended	31 March 2017	31 March 2016
	£	£
Trading profit (loss)	(41,250)	10,680
Chargeable gain (loss)	(5,650)	15,400
Rental profit	12,000	12,000
Gift aid	1,800	1,800

Tulip Limited has a policy of always claiming relief for losses as soon as possible.

Complete the following table to show how Tulip Limited would claim for their losses.

	£
How much trading loss can be claimed against income in the year ended 31 March 2017?	
How much trading loss can be claimed against income in the year ended 31 March 2016?	
How much trading loss can be carried forward to the year ended 31 March 2018?	
How much capital loss can be carried forward against capital gains in the year ended 31 March 2018?	
How much gift aid can be set against income in the year ended 31 March 2016?	
How much gift aid can be set against income in the year ended 31 March 2017?	
How much gift aid can be carried forward to be set against income in the year ended 31 March 2018?	

Task 9

You work for a firm of accountants. An enquiry has been received from a client. The client is the Managing Director of a limited company that employs 50 people, and has just completed its first year of business. The company manufactures various components for the energy generation sector, and is also developing a new method of utilising tidal power to generate renewable energy. This project satisfies the HMRC definition to claim research and development tax relief.

The company spent £500,000 on qualifying development revenue costs, and after claiming R&D allowance, is likely to incur a tax loss of about £1,250,000, on turnover of £2,000,000. The company has no other income. The company's assets are £15 million.

It is expected that the company will be profitable by the third operating year.

The client wishes to understand the allowances that will be claimed, and what options are available for claiming and offsetting the first year loss. He also wants to be provided with a recommendation for how the loss should be dealt with to generate the earliest cash flow advantage.

Answer the client's enquiry, including relevant calculations, using the space provided below.

Task 10

(a)   Dickinson Limited sold an asset in April 2016 for £43,500. The costs of disposal were £300. The asset was bought in August 2000 for £19,850 plus buying costs of £650.

The indexation factor from August 2000 to April 2016 is 0.533.

Calculate the chargeable gain on the disposal of this asset using the following table. Enter zero against any costs that are not allowable.

	£	£
Proceeds		
Disposal costs		
Cost		
Buying costs		
Indexation allowance		
Gain		

(b)   Indicate whether each of the following statements is true or false.

	True	False
(a) Indexation allowance does not apply to individuals under CGT		
(b) A limited company can set an annual exempt amount against its gains		

Task 11

(a)   Neil bought 3,000 shares in Crossfield Limited in April 1998 for £3 each. In July 2002 there was a bonus issue of 1 for 3 shares. Neil sold 800 shares in the company in August 2003. In January 2012 Neil bought a further 5,000 shares for a total of £23,200.

In June 2016 Neil sold 2,500 shares in Crossfield Limited for a total of £14,850.

Calculate the chargeable gain on the sale of the shares in June 2016. Show the number and cost of the shares still held at that time in your workings.

(b) Two taxpayers each made a capital gain in 2016/17 of £35,000 (not residential property) before deducting their annual exempt amount. The amount of their taxable income (after deducting their personal allowance) is shown in the table below.

Calculate the amount of capital gains tax payable (in whole pounds) by each individual using the following table.

Taxpayer	Taxable income £	Gains chargeable at 10% £	Gains chargeable at 20% £	Total CGT payable £
Sonia	18,500			
Steve	41,250			

Practice assessment 3

Task 1

(a) Analyse the tax treatment of the following items in a sole trader's trading income computation by ticking the appropriate column.

		Add back to net profit	Deduct from net profit	No adjustment required
(a)	Bank interest receivable			
(b)	Bank interest payable			
(c)	Increase in general provision for irrecoverable debts			
(d)	Profit on sale of non-current assets			
(e)	Staff travelling expenses			
(f)	Owner's class 2 & 4 NIC			
(g)	Discounts receivable			

(b) Lemming Limited has the following statement of profit or loss:

	£	£
Gross profit		1,980,560
Wages and salaries	863,200	
Accountancy and legal costs	48,450	
Motor expenses	121,680	
Repairs and renewals	130,500	
Office expenses	82,600	
Depreciation	245,110	
Other expenses	88,840	1,580,380
Profit		400,180

Notes include:

Wages and salaries include:

Directors' salaries and personal pension contributions	£175,000

Accountancy and legal costs include:

Legal fees to renew 10 year lease on office building	£4,120
Taxation advice	£3,550
Annual accountancy and audit fee	£11,200

Motor expenses include:

Operating lease of 180 g/km car used for business by Director (50% private use)	£9,860

Repairs and renewals include:

Replacement of office furniture	£12,000

Capital allowances have been calculated as	£33,780

Complete the following computation. You may not need to use all the lines provided.

	£
Profit	400,180
Disallowed items added back:	
Allowed items deducted:	
Adjusted trading profits	

(c) Cherie started trading on 1 February 2015. She makes up her accounts to 31 December. The profits were calculated as:

	£
Period to 31 December 2015	93,500
Year to 31 December 2016	84,000
Year to 31 December 2017	60,000

Complete the following table by inserting tax years and taxable profits together with the amount of any overlap profits.

	Tax year	Amount £
First year of trading		
Second year of trading		
Third year of trading		
Overlap profits		

Task 2

(a)　Adam, Ben and Clive have been in partnership for many years, sharing profits in the ratio 5:3:2. They have always made their accounts up to 31 December each year.

On 31 May 2016, Clive left the partnership. On 1 June 2016 Catherine joined the partnership, and all the partners then agreed to divide their profits equally.

For the year ended 31 December 2016, the partnership trading profit was £360,000.

For the year ended 31 December 2017, the partnership trading profit was £396,000.

Clive had no overlap profits brought forward.

(1)　Using the following table, calculate the division of profits between the partners for the accounting year ended 31 December 2016.

	Total £	Adam £	Ben £	Clive £	Catherine £
Period to 31 May					
Period from 1 June					
Total					

(2)　Insert the assessable profits for each partner for the tax year 2016/17 into the following table.

	Assessable profits £
Adam	
Ben	
Clive	
Catherine	

(b)　Calculate Ben's National Insurance Contributions for 2016/17. Round answers to the nearest penny.

	£
Class 2 NIC	
Class 4 NIC at 9%	
Class 4 NIC at 2%	

Task 3

A company has the following information regarding its non-current assets for an 8-month CAP ending on 30/4/2016.

	£
Written down values brought forward:	
General (main) pool	125,000
Special rate pool	47,000
Additions:	
Computer System (bought December 2015)	371,666
New car for Sales Director (emissions 170 g/km)	28,000
Disposals:	
Machinery	5,000

Calculate the total capital allowances and show the balances to carry forward to the next accounting period.

Task 4

Bryson Limited has a 12-month CAP ending on 31/12/2016.

It has the following tax adjusted results for that period:

Trading Profits	£1,830,000
Trading Loss brought forward	£130,000
Rental Income	£110,000
Chargeable Gains	£89,000
Capital Loss brought forward	£13,000

Complete, as far as possible, the following extract from the CT600 form for Bryson Limited.

Tax calculation
Turnover

| 145 | Total turnover from trade | £ ⬜⬜⬜⬜⬜⬜⬜⬜⬜⬜⬜⬜⬜⬜ . 0 0 |

| 150 | Banks, building societies, insurance companies and other financial concerns –
put an 'X' in this box if you do not have a recognised turnover and have not made an entry in box 145 | ⬜ |

Income

| 155 | Trading profits | £ ⬜⬜⬜⬜⬜⬜⬜⬜⬜ . 0 0 |

| 160 | Trading losses brought forward claimed against profits | £ ⬜⬜⬜⬜⬜⬜⬜⬜⬜ . 0 0 |

| 165 | Net trading profits – *box 155 minus box 160* | £ ⬜⬜⬜⬜⬜⬜⬜⬜⬜ . 0 0 |

| 170 | Bank, building society or other interest, and profits
from non-trading loan relationships | £ ⬜⬜⬜⬜⬜⬜⬜⬜⬜ . 0 0 |

| 172 | Put an 'X' in box 172 if the figure in box 170 is net of
carrying back a deficit from a later accounting period | ⬜ |

| 175 | Annual payments not otherwise charged to Corporation Tax
and from which Income Tax has not been deducted | £ ⬜⬜⬜⬜⬜⬜⬜⬜⬜ . 0 0 |

Income *continued*

180 Non-exempt dividends or distributions from non–UK resident companies

£ ⬚ · 0 0

185 Income from which Income Tax has been deducted

£ ⬚ · 0 0

190 Income from a property business

£ ⬚ · 0 0

195 Non-trading gains on intangible fixed assets

£ ⬚ · 0 0

200 Tonnage Tax profits

£ ⬚ · 0 0

205 Income not falling under any other heading

£ ⬚ · 0 0

Chargeable gains

210 Gross chargeable gains

£ ⬚ · 0 0

215 Allowable losses including losses brought forward

£ ⬚ · 0 0

220 Net chargeable gains - *box 210 minus box 215*

£ ⬚ · 0 0

Profits before deductions and reliefs

225 Losses brought forward against certain investment income

£ ⬚ · 0 0

230 Non-trade deficits on loan relationships (including interest) and derivative contracts (financial instruments) brought forward

£ ⬚ · 0 0

235 Profits before other deductions and reliefs – *net sum of boxes 165 to 205 and 220 minus sum of boxes 225 and 230*

£ ⬚ · 0 0

Task 5

(a)   Florinda Limited has produced the following results for the 17-month accounting period to 31 December 2016.

Trading Profits for 17-month period		
(before capital allowances)		£714,000
Capital Allowances:	y/e 31/7/2016	£74,000
	5 months to 31/12/2016	£41,000
Chargeable Gains:	Disposal 12/12/2015	£33,000
	Disposal 19/6/2016	(£44,000) loss
	Disposal 10/11/2016	£17,000
Rental Income – monthly amount		£3,100
Gift Aid Payment (paid 31/12/2016)		£6,000

Use the following table to calculate the TTP for each CAP.

	CAP 12 months to 31/7/2016 £	CAP 5 months to 31/12/2016 £
Trading Profits before CAs		
Capital Allowances		
Trading Profits		
Chargeable Gains		
Rental Income		
Sub total		
Gift Aid		
TTP		

(b)   Calculate the Corporation Tax payable by Florinda Limited for the two accounting periods. Show your answer in whole pounds.

	CAP 12 months to 31/7/2016 £	CAP 5 months to 31/12/2016 £
Corporation Tax Payable		

Task 6

(a)   Alison has been trading for many years, and her Income Tax and NIC liability is as follows:

2013/14	£19,250
2014/15	£18,400
2015/16	£21,500

Alison has not made any claim to reduce payments on account.

Complete the following table to show the total amounts that Alison will pay on the dates shown.

Payment date	Amount £
31 July 2016	
31 January 2017	
31 July 2017	

(b)   Cannie Limited has an accounting year end of 31 May 2016. The final date for submission of the CT600 tax return is:

Task 7

(a)   Identify whether each of the following statements is true or false.

		True	False
(a)	Interest is payable by self-employed individuals on underpayments of amounts due on account, but not on balancing payments		
(b)	A total late submission penalty is payable for self-employed individuals of £1,000 for tax returns late by six months		
(c)	Online returns have later submission deadlines than paper-based returns for individuals		
(d)	A late payment of the balancing payment of between 30 days and six months will incur a penalty of 5% of the tax due		
(e)	A tax advisor is liable for a £3,000 penalty if they assist in making an incorrect return		
(f)	Companies must notify HMRC within three months of starting to trade		

(b)   Guy Collins Limited made a prompted disclosure of an error which was considered deliberate, but not concealed. The additional Corporation Tax payable as a result was £40,500. The penalty will be as follows:

Minimum £	
Maximum £	

Task 8

A limited company has the following tax-adjusted results for the 12-month CAPs ending on 31 December:

	2015	2016	2017
	£	£	£
Trading profits	120,500	0	375,000
Trading loss		85,000	
Chargeable gain	50,300		
Capital loss		20,100	
Rental income	10,800	12,400	14,200

Assuming that the company wishes to claim any loss relief as early as possible, complete the following table. Insert zeros into any cells that do not apply.

	2015	2016	2017
	£	£	£
Trading profits			
Trading loss offset against trading profits only			
Net chargeable gains			
Rental income			
Trading loss offset against taxable total profits			
Taxable total profits after offsetting losses			

Task 9

You work for a small firm of accountants. One of your clients is a self-employed car dealer, and an additional rate taxpayer. He has arrived for a meeting that he requested.

He explains that he has been introduced by a friend at his golf club to a tax consultant who has recommended that he joins a tax avoidance scheme. The tax advisor has told him that this will reduce his normal tax liability by a substantial amount, and that it must be legal since HMRC is aware of the scheme.

The client is keen to go ahead, and asks you to explain the differences between tax avoidance and tax evasion, and any implications of joining the scheme. He also requests details of other clients that have considered or joined such schemes.

Give your response in the box below, under the headings given. Include consideration of the ethical implications for you and your practice.

Tax avoidance and tax evasion

Implications of joining the scheme

Details of other clients

Ethical implications for you and your practice

Task 10

(a)   Analyse the following assets into those that are chargeable regarding CGT and those that are exempt.

	Chargeable	Exempt
Disposals to connected persons		
Plant and machinery sold at a gain		
Cars		
Gifts to charities		

(b)   Response Limited bought a chattel in April 1998 for £4,000. The item was sold in April 2016 for £9,000, less sales commission of 5%.

The indexation factor from April 1998 to April 2016 is 0.608.

Complete the following table to calculate the chargeable gain.

	Amount £
Sale proceeds	
Sales commission	
Net sales proceeds	
Cost	
Indexation	
Provisional gain	
Chattel restriction	
Final gain	

(c)   Mary Poole is a sole trader who pays tax at the higher rate. She purchased a warehouse in October 2000 for £460,000, and sold it in September 2016 for £700,000. She then purchased a shop in December 2017 for £550,000.

(1)   Complete the following table relating to the gain on the sale of the warehouse, and deferral of that gain (if any). This was her only capital gain in 2016/17. Assume the gain does not qualify for entrepreneurs' relief.

	£
Sale proceeds	
Cost	
Total gain	
Deferred gain	
Gain chargeable immediately	
Annual exempt amount	
Capital Gains Tax payable	

(2)   The cost of the shop will be deemed to be £ [   ] when it is ultimately sold.

Task 11

Bee Ltd bought 5,000 shares in Wye Ltd for £15,900 in October 2001. Bonus shares were issued in April 2002 at 1 for 10. A purchase of 2,000 shares was made on 20 April 2016 for £4.80 per share. On 25 April 2016 Bee Ltd sold 3,000 of the shares for £4.95 per share.

Indexation factors were:

October 2001 to April 2016: 0.500

Clearly showing the matching of the shares, calculate the gain or loss on the sale of shares and any pool balances remaining.

Answers to practice assessment 1

Task 1

(a)   **(a)** and **(f)** Allow (no action); **(b)**, **(c)** and **(e)** Disallow and add back; **(d)** Disallow and deduct

(b)

Tax year (YYYY/YY)	Basis period start date (DD/MM/YY)	Basis period end date (DD/MM/YY)	Profits £	Total overlap profits £
2015/16	06/04/15	05/04/16	38,400	
2016/17	01/05/15	30/04/16	38,400	
				35,200

Task 2

(a)

To 31 October 2016	Molly £	Nigel £
Share of profits	38,472	25,648
From 1 November 2016	**Molly £**	**Nigel £**
Interest on capital	800	300
Salary	5,000	7,500
Share of profits	17,710	14,490

(b)

	£
Class 2 NIC	145.60
Class 4 NIC at 9%	3,144.60
Class 4 NIC at 2%	379.64

Task 3

CAP FOR THE 12 MONTHS TO 30/6/2016			
	Main pool	**Special rate pool**	**Capital allowances**
	£	£	£
WDV bf	105,000	17,000	
add			
Acquisitions with FYAs:			
Low emission car £25,000			
100% FYA £(25,000)			25,000
	0		
Acquisitions qualifying for AIA:			
Computer £290,000			
AIA claimed* £(100,000)			100,000
Excess	190,000		
less			
Proceeds of Disposals	(5,000)		
	290,000	17,000	
WDA	(52,200)	(1,360)	53,560
WDV cf	237,800	15,640	
Total Capital Allowances			178,560

*AIA limit (£500,000 x 6/12) + (£200,000 x 6/12) = £350,000, but limited to £100,000 (6/12 x £200,000) for expenditure on or after 1/1/2016

Task 4

PARTNERSHIP STATEMENT (SHORT) for the year ended 5 April 2016

Please read these instructions before completing the Statement

Use these pages to allocate partnership income if the only income for the relevant return period was trading and professional income or taxed interest and alternative finance receipts from banks and building societies. Otherwise you must download or ask the SA Orderline for the 'Partnership Statement (Full)' pages to record details of the allocation of all the partnership income. Go to www.gov.uk/self-assessment-forms-and-helpsheets

Step 1 Fill in boxes 1 to 29 and boxes A and B as appropriate. Get the figures you need from the relevant boxes in the Partnership Tax Return. Complete a separate Statement for each accounting period covered by this Partnership Tax Return and for each trade or profession carried on by the partnership.

Step 2 Then allocate the amounts in boxes 11 to 29 attributable to each partner using the allocation columns on this page and page 7, read the Partnership Tax Return Guide, go to www.gov.uk/self-assessment-forms-and-helpsheets
If the partnership has more than 3 partners, please photocopy page 7.

Step 3 Each partner will need a copy of their allocation of income to fill in their personal tax return.

PARTNERSHIP INFORMATION
If the partnership business includes a trade or profession, enter here the accounting period for which appropriate items in this statement are returned.

Start **1** 1 / 4 / 16

End **2** 31 / 3 / 17

Nature of trade **3** Wholesale Fabric

MIXED PARTNERSHIPS

Tick here if this Statement is drawn up using Corporation Tax rules **4**

Tick here if this Statement is drawn up using tax rules for non-residents **5**

Individual partner details

6 Name of partner   Alison Amsterdam

Address

Postcode

Date appointed as a partner (if during 2014–15 or 2015–16)
7 / /

Date ceased to be a partner (if during 2014–15 or 2015–16)
9 / /

Partner's Unique Taxpayer Reference (UTR)
8

Partner's National Insurance number
10

Partnership's profits, losses, income, tax credits, etc

Tick this box if the items entered in the box had foreign tax taken off

Partner's share of profits, losses, income, tax credits, etc

Copy figures in boxes 11 to 29 to boxes in the individual's **Partnership (short)** pages as shown below

- **for an accounting period ended in 2015–16** ▼

from box 3.83 Profit from a trade or profession	**A**	**11** £ 80,000	Profit **11** £ 48,000	Copy this figure to box 8
from box 3.82 Adjustment on change of basis		**11A** £	**11A** £	Copy this figure to box 10
from box 3.84 Loss from a trade or profession	**B**	**12** £	Loss **12** £	Copy this figure to box 8
from box 10.4 Business Premises Renovation Allowance		**12A** £	**12A** £	Copy this figure to box 15

- **for the period 6 April 2015 to 5 April 2016***

from box 7.9A UK taxed interest and taxed alternative finance receipts	**22** £ 1,600	**22** £ 960	Copy this figure to box 28
from box 3.97 CIS deductions made by contractors on account of tax	**24** £	**24** £	Copy this figure to box 30
from box 3.98 Other tax taken off trading income	**24A** £	**24A** £	Copy this figure to box 31
from box 7.8A Income Tax taken off	**25** £	**25** £	Copy this figure to box 29
from box 3.117 Partnership charges	**29** £	**29** £	Copy this figure to box 4, 'Other tax reliefs' section on page Ai 2 in your personal tax return

* if you are a 'CT Partnership' see the Partnership Tax Return Guide

Task 5

(a)

	CAP 12 months to 31/8/2016 £	CAP 4 months to 31/12/2016 £
Trading Profits before CAs	600,000	200,000
Capital Allowances	54,000	19,000
Trading Profits	546,000	181,000
Chargeable Gains	50,000	41,000
Rental Income	24,000	8,000
Sub total	620,000	230,000
Gift Aid	0	6,000
TTP	620,000	224,000

(b)

	CAP 12 months to 31/8/2016 £	CAP 4 months to 31/12/2016 £
Corporation Tax Payable	124,000	44,800

Task 6

(a)

Tax year (YYYY/YY)	Payment date (DD/MM/YYYY)	Payment on account / Balancing payment	Amount £
2015/16	31/01/2017	Balancing payment	1,200
2016/17	31/01/2017	Payment on account	9,650
2016/17	31/07/2017	Payment on account	9,650

(b)   1 June 2017

Task 7

(a)   **(b)** is False; the remaining statements are True

(b)

Minimum £	0
Maximum £	450

Task 8   **(a)**, **(e)**, **(f)** and **(g)** are True; **(b)**, **(c)** and **(d)** are False

Task 9

The Corporation Tax Return (CT600) for the year ended 31 December 2015 should have been filed by 31 December 2016. The penalty for submitting over three months late is £200. If the return is now submitted promptly it should avoid a further penalty which could be imposed of 10% of the Corporation Tax (ie £4,500) for submissions over six months late.

The final payment of Corporation Tax for the year ended 31 December 2015 should have been made by 1 October 2016. Interest will be payable (currently at 3%) from that date until payment is made. The company is not liable to make instalment payments, since this is its first year of trading.

There is a penalty for failing to keep appropriate records. This is up to £3,000 per chargeable accounting period. Provided the missing records only relate to 2015 then only one penalty of £3,000 may be charged.

Looking forward, the tax return for the year ended 31 December 2016 should be filed by 31 December 2017, with the tax payment made by 1 October 2017.

Task 10

(a)

	Chargeable	Exempt
Government Stocks (gilts)		✔
Shares in Limited Companies	✔	
Trading Inventory		✔
Land	✔	

(b)   Proceeds: £7,100

Cost: £4,000

Indexation allowance: £2,132

Gain: £968

Chattel restriction on gain: £1,833

No. The chattel restriction will not have any effect on the original gain.

Task 11

(a)

	No. Shares	Cost £	Indexed Cost £
Purchase October 2001	9,000	27,900	27,900
Bonus shares	900	0	0
Indexation to July 2003			3,181
Purchase July 2003	5,000	19,000	19,000
Sub total	14,900	46,900	50,081
Indexation to April 2016			22,136
Total	14,900	46,900	72,217
Disposal	(10,000)	(31,477)	(48,468)
Pool Balance	4,900	15,423	23,749

Proceeds	£50,000
Indexed Cost	£48,468
Gain	£1,532

(b)   **(1)**   The **loss** on the sale of shares on 12 January 2017 is **£1,580**.

(2)   The **gain** on the sale of shares on 31 March 2017 is **£9,500**.

Answers to practice assessment 2

Task 1

(a)

	£
Profit	336,875
Disallowed items added back:	
Lisa's salary and personal pension contributions	75,400
Legal fees to purchase new office building	10,250
Operating lease of 180 g/km car used for business	1,749
Expenses of Lisa's car which is used 70% for the business	3,750
Depreciation	155,310
Allowed items deducted:	
Capital allowances	21,380
Adjusted trading profits	561,954

(b)   **(a)** and **(b)** Add back to profit; **(c)** No adjustment required; **(d)** Deduct from profit

(c)

Tax year	Basis period start date	Basis period end date	Profits	Total overlap profits
(YYYY/YY)	(DD/MM/YY)	(DD/MM/YY)	£	£
2016/17	01/07/15	30/06/16	49,800	
2017/18	01/05/16	30/04/17	52,700	
				11,300

Task 2

(a)

To 31 August 2016	Olly £	Pete £
Share of profits	19,200	19,200
From 1 September 2016	**Olly £**	**Pete £**
Interest on capital	875	700
Salary	8,750	7,000
Share of profits	14,574	21,861

(b)

	Profits £	Class 4 at 9% £	Class 4 at 2% £	Total Class 4 NIC £
Brian	49,280.00	3,144.60	125.60	3,270.20
Colin	40,320.00	2,903.40	0	2,903.40

Task 3

Period ended 31 December 2016		General pool £	Special rate pool £	Capital allowances £
WDV bf		157,500	31,680	
Additions FYA	29,500			
100% FYA	(29,500)	0		29,500
Additions AIA				
Machinery	139,334			
AIA (£200,000 x 7/12)	(116,667)			116,667
		22,667		
Sub totals		180,167	31,680	
WDA 18% x 7/12		(18,918)		18,918
WDA 8% x 7/12			(1,478)	1,478
WDV cf		161,249	30,202	
Capital Allowances				166,563
Period ended 30 April 2017				
WDV bf		161,249	30,202	
Disposal proceeds		(55,500)	(22,100)	
		(19,800)		
Balancing allowances		(85,949)	(8,102)	94,051
WDV cf		0	0	
Capital Allowances				94,051

Task 4

Tax calculation

Turnover

145	Total turnover from trade	£	4 1 5 0 3 0 0 · 0 0

| 150 | Banks, building societies, insurance companies and other financial concerns – *put an 'X' in this box if you do not have a recognised turnover and have not made an entry in box 145* | |

Income

155	Trading profits	£	1 1 3 0 4 5 0 · 0 0

| 160 | Trading losses brought forward claimed against profits | £ | 3 5 9 5 0 0 · 0 0 |

| 165 | Net trading profits – *box 155 minus box 160* | £ | 7 7 0 9 5 0 · 0 0 |

| 170 | Bank, building society or other interest, and profits from non-trading loan relationships | £ | · 0 0 |

| 172 | Put an 'X' in box 172 if the figure in box 170 is net of carrying back a deficit from a later accounting period | |

| 175 | Annual payments not otherwise charged to Corporation Tax and from which Income Tax has not been deducted | £ | · 0 0 |

Income *continued*

180	Non-exempt dividends or distributions from non–UK resident companies	£	· 0 0

| 185 | Income from which Income Tax has been deducted | £ | · 0 0 |

| 190 | Income from a property business | £ | 4 4 5 6 3 0 · 0 0 |

| 195 | Non-trading gains on intangible fixed assets | £ | · 0 0 |

| 200 | Tonnage Tax profits | £ | · 0 0 |

| 205 | Income not falling under any other heading | £ | · 0 0 |

Chargeable gains

210	Gross chargeable gains	£	8 5 6 9 5 · 0 0

| 215 | Allowable losses including losses brought forward | £ | 8 5 6 9 5 · 0 0 |

| 220 | Net chargeable gains – *box 210 minus box 215* | £ | 0 · 0 0 |

Profits before deductions and reliefs

225	Losses brought forward against certain investment income	£	· 0 0

| 230 | Non-trade deficits on loan relationships (including interest) and derivative contracts (financial instruments) brought forward | £ | · 0 0 |

| 235 | Profits before other deductions and reliefs – *net sum of boxes 165 to 205 and 220 minus sum of boxes 225 and 230* | £ | 1 2 1 6 5 8 0 · 0 0 |

Task 5

(a)

	First accounting period £	Second accounting period £
Capital gains	5,510	19,475
Trading profits	113,556	47,315

(b)

	CAP 12 months to 30/9/2016 £	CAP 5 months to 28/2/2017 £
Corporation Tax Payable	23,813	13,358

Task 6

(a)

Payment date	Amount £
31 July 2016	7,725
31 January 2017	4,800
31 July 2017	6,750

(b)   1 May 2017

Task 7

(a)   **(a)**, **(c)** and **(d)** are False; **(b)**, **(e)** and **(f)** are True

(b)

Minimum £	675
Maximum £	1,350

Task 8

	£
How much trading loss can be claimed against income in the year ended 31 March 2017?	12,000
How much trading loss can be claimed against income in the year ended 31 March 2016?	29,250
How much trading loss can be carried forward to the year ended 31 March 2018?	0
How much capital loss can be carried forward against capital gains in the year ended 31 March 2018?	5,650
How much gift aid can be set against income in the year ended 31 March 2016?	1,800
How much gift aid can be set against income in the year ended 31 March 2017?	0
How much gift aid can be carried forward to be set against income in the year ended 31 March 2018?	0

Task 9

The company qualifies as a small / medium sized company since it has fewer than 500 employees, turnover less than 100 million euros and assets of under 86 million euros. This means that allowable R&D expenditure on qualifying projects will be 230% of actual R&D expenditure. In this case the amount of £1,150,000 will have been used as allowable costs instead of the actual cost of £500,000.

The likely loss of £1,250,000 cannot be set against the taxable total profits of the current year, as there are none. The only option of the traditional loss relief methods would be to carry the loss forward to set against future profits from the same trade. As this is likely to be in the third year of trading this would have serious cash-flow implications.

As this is a company with qualifying R&D expenditure there is a further loss option available. Losses can be surrendered (within limits) in exchange for tax credits of 14.5% of the surrendered amount. In this case the loss that could be surrendered would be limited to the R&D relief claimed of £1,150,000. This would generate tax credits of £1,150,000 x 14.5% = £166,750.

It is therefore recommended that the maximum available of £1,150,000 loss be surrendered in exchange for tax credits which will be immediately available for repayment by HMRC, easing cash flow. Note that the amount of tax credit will probably be less than the tax relief by carrying the loss forward (depending on future tax rates).

The balance of £100,000 loss can then be carried forward against the first available profits of the same trade in the future.

Task 10

(a)

	£	£
Proceeds		43,500
Disposal costs		300
Cost	19,850	
Buying costs	650	
Indexation allowance	10,927	
Gain		11,773

(b)   **(a)** True; **(b)** False

Task 11

(a)

		Number of shares	Cost of shares £
April 1998	Purchase	3,000	9,000
July 2002	Bonus issue	1,000	0
		4,000	9,000
August 2003	Disposal	(800)	(1,800)
		3,200	7,200
January 2012	Purchase	5,000	23,200
		8,200	30,400
June 2016	Disposal	(2,500)	(9,268)
	Balance	5,700	21,132
	Proceeds	14,850	
	Cost	9,268	
	Gain	5,582	

(b)

Taxpayer	Taxable income £	Gains chargeable at 10% £	Gains chargeable at 20% £	Total CGT payable £
Sonia	18,500	13,500	10,400	3,430
Steve	41,250	0	23,900	4,780

Answers to practice assessment 3

Task 1

(a) **(a)** and **(d)** Deduct from net profit; **(b)**, **(e)** and **(g)** No adjustment required; **(c)** and **(f)** Add back to net profit

(b)

	£
Profit	400,180
Disallowed items added back:	
Operating lease of 180 g/km car	1,479
Replacement of office furniture	12,000
Depreciation	245,110
Allowed items deducted:	
Capital allowances	33,780
Adjusted trading profits	624,989

(c)

	Tax year	Amount £
First year of trading	2014/15	17,000
Second year of trading[(1)]	2015/16	100,500
Third year of trading	2016/17	84,000
Overlap profits[(2)]		24,000

Workings:

(1) 1/2/15 - 31/1/16 £93,500 + (£84,000 x 1/12) = £100,500

(2) (1/2/15 - 5/4/15) + (1/1/16-31/1/16) = (£17,000 + £7,000) = £24,000

Task 2

(a)   (1)

	Total	Adam	Ben	Clive	Catherine
	£	£	£	£	£
Period to 31 May	150,000	75,000	45,000	30,000	0
Period from 1 June	210,000	70,000	70,000	0	70,000
Total	360,000	145,000	115,000	30,000	70,000

(2)

	Assessable profits £
Adam	145,000
Ben	115,000
Clive	30,000
Catherine	103,000

Note: Catherine's assessable profits are based on the period 1 June 2016 - 5 April 2017:
£70,000 + (£396,000 / 3 x 3/12) = £103,000

(b)

	£
Class 2 NIC	145.60
Class 4 NIC at 9%	3,144.60
Class 4 NIC at 2%	1,440.00

Task 3

	Main pool	Special rate pool	Capital allowances
	£	£	£
WDV bf	125,000	47,000	
Additions without FYA or AIA:			
Car		28,000	
Additions qualifying for AIA:			
Computer system			
371,666			
AIA* (233,333)			233,333
	138,333		
Disposals	(5,000)		
	258,333	75,000	
WDA 18% x 8/12	(31,000)		31,000
WDA 8% x 8/12		(4,000)	4,000
WDV cf	227,333	71,000	
Total Capital Allowances			268,333

*Maximum AIA: (£500,000 x 4/12) + (£200,000 x 4/12) = £233,333

Task 4

Tax calculation

Turnover

145 Total turnover from trade   £ ⬚⬚⬚⬚⬚⬚⬚⬚⬚⬚⬚⬚⬚⬚⬚ · 0 0

150 Banks, building societies, insurance companies and other financial concerns –
put an 'X' in this box if you do not have a recognised turnover and have not made an entry in box 145   ⬚

Income

155 Trading profits   £ 1 8 3 0 0 0 0 · 0 0

160 Trading losses brought forward claimed against profits   £ 1 3 0 0 0 0 · 0 0

165 Net trading profits – *box 155 minus box 160*   £ 1 7 0 0 0 0 0 · 0 0

170 Bank, building society or other interest, and profits
from non-trading loan relationships   £ ⬚⬚⬚⬚⬚⬚⬚⬚ · 0 0

172 Put an 'X' in box 172 if the figure in box 170 is net of
carrying back a deficit from a later accounting period   ⬚

175 Annual payments not otherwise charged to Corporation Tax
and from which Income Tax has not been deducted   £ ⬚⬚⬚⬚⬚⬚⬚⬚ · 0 0

Income *continued*

180 Non-exempt dividends or distributions from
non–UK resident companies   £ ⬚⬚⬚⬚⬚⬚⬚ · 0 0

185 Income from which Income Tax has been deducted   £ ⬚⬚⬚⬚⬚⬚⬚ · 0 0

190 Income from a property business   £ 1 1 0 0 0 0 · 0 0

195 Non-trading gains on intangible fixed assets   £ ⬚⬚⬚⬚⬚⬚⬚ · 0 0

200 Tonnage Tax profits   £ ⬚⬚⬚⬚⬚⬚⬚ · 0 0

205 Income not falling under any other heading   £ ⬚⬚⬚⬚⬚⬚⬚ · 0 0

Chargeable gains

210 Gross chargeable gains   £ 8 9 0 0 0 · 0 0

215 Allowable losses including losses brought forward   £ 1 3 0 0 0 · 0 0

220 Net chargeable gains – *box 210 minus box 215*   £ 7 6 0 0 0 · 0 0

Profits before deductions and reliefs

225 Losses brought forward against certain investment income   £ ⬚⬚⬚⬚⬚⬚⬚ · 0 0

230 Non-trade deficits on loan relationships (including interest)
and derivative contracts (financial instruments)
brought forward   £ ⬚⬚⬚⬚⬚⬚⬚ · 0 0

235 Profits before other deductions and reliefs – *net sum of
boxes 165 to 205 and 220 minus sum of boxes 225 and 230*   £ 1 8 8 6 0 0 0 · 0 0

Task 5

(a)

	CAP 12 months to 31/7/2016	CAP 5 months to 31/12/2016
	£	£
Trading Profits before CAs	504,000	210,000
Capital Allowances	74,000	41,000
Trading Profits	430,000	169,000
Chargeable Gains	0	6,000
Rental Income	37,200	15,500
Sub total	467,200	190,500
Gift Aid	0	6,000
TTP	467,200	184,500

(b)

	CAP 12 months to 31/7/2016	CAP 5 months to 31/12/2016
	£	£
Corporation Tax Payable	93,440	36,900

Task 6

(a)

Payment date	Amount
	£
31 July 2016	9,200
31 January 2017	13,850
31 July 2017	10,750

(b)   31 May 2017

Task 7

(a)   **(a)** is False; the remaining statements are True

(b)

Minimum £	14,175
Maximum £	28,350

Task 8

	2015	2016	2017
	£	£	£
Trading profits	120,500	0	375,000
Trading loss offset against trading profits only	0	0	0
Net chargeable gains	50,300	0	0
Rental income	10,800	12,400	14,200
Trading loss offset against taxable total profits	72,600	12,400	0
Taxable total profits after offsetting losses	109,000	0	389,200

Task 9

> **Tax avoidance and tax evasion**
>
> Tax avoidance is the legal use of claims and allowances to reduce the amount of tax payable. Tax evasion involves using illegal methods to reduce tax. There is a grey area between these two activities, and it is not always clear how HMRC or the courts will define a particular activity or scheme.
>
> Where a scheme relies on concealment, pretence, non-disclosure or misrepresentation, this would be categorised as tax evasion which can result in criminal prosecution. 'Aggressive' tax avoidance schemes may also be examined under the recent General Anti-Abuse Rule (GAAR) legislation which will consider whether the law is being used in the way that Parliament originally anticipated.
>
> **Implications of joining the scheme**
>
> If HMRC are aware of a particular scheme it does not mean that they have approved it as being legal. There could be ongoing investigations into the scheme which could result in it being declared illegal. Taxpayers must disclose their use of avoidance schemes, and will consequently be viewed as high risk individuals by HMRC. Their tax affairs may be subject to more scrutiny as a result.
>
> **Details of other clients**
>
> Details of other clients should not be provided as this would be a breach of confidentiality.
>
> **Ethical implications for you and your practice**
>
> Accountants should also consider their own ethical position when clients wish to undertake tax avoidance, and distance themselves from situations that do not meet their own or their professional body's ethical standards. They must also consider any reputational damage that may occur as a result of facilitating their clients' involvement in particular schemes.

Task 10

(a)

	Chargeable	Exempt
Disposals to connected persons	✔	
Plant and machinery sold at a gain	✔	
Cars		✔
Gifts to charities		✔

(b)

	Amount £
Sale proceeds	9,000
Sales commission	450
Net sales proceeds	8,550
Cost	4,000
Indexation	2,432
Provisional gain	2,118
Chattel restriction	5,000
Final gain	2,118

(c)

(1)

	£
Sale proceeds	700,000
Cost	460,000
Total gain	240,000
Deferred gain	90,000
Gain chargeable immediately	150,000
Annual exempt amount	11,100
Capital Gains Tax payable	27,780

(2)   The cost of the shop will be deemed to be **£460,000** when it is ultimately sold.

Task 11

Matching shares bought 20 April 2016	£		
Proceeds (2,000)	9,900		
Cost	9,600		
Gain	300		
Share pool	No	£	£
October 2001 purchase	5,000	15,900	15,900
Bonus shares	500		
Indexation			7,950
Sub total	5,500	15,900	23,850
Disposal	(1,000)	(2,891)	(4,336)
Pool balance	4,500	13,009	19,514
Matching with pool	£		
Proceeds (1,000)	4,950		
Indexed cost	4,336		
Gain	614		
Total gain	914		

Reference Material

for AAT Assessment of Business Tax

Finance Act 2016

For assessments from 1 January – 31 December 2017

Note: this reference material is accessible by candidates during their live computer-based assessment for Business Tax.

This material was current at the time this book was published, but may be subject to change. Readers are advised to check the AAT website or Osborne Books website for any updates.

Reference material for AAT assessment of Business Tax

Introduction
This document comprises data that you may need to consult during your Business Tax computer-based assessment. The material can be consulted during the sample and live assessments through pop-up windows. It is made available here so you can familiarise yourself with the content before the test.

Do not take a print of this document into the exam room with you. Unless you need a printed version as part of reasonable adjustments for particular needs, in which case you must discuss this with your tutor at least six weeks before the assessment date.

This document may be changed to reflect periodical updates in the computer-based assessment, so please check you have the most recent version while studying. This version is based on Finance Act 2016 and is for use in AAT assessments 1 January – 31 December 2017.

Taxation tables for business tax – 2016/17

Capital allowances

Annual investment allowance	
From 1 / 6 April 2014	£500,000
From 1 January 2016	£200,000
Plant and machinery writing down allowance	
Long life assets and integral features	8%
Other assets	18%
Motor cars	
CO_2 emissions up to 75 g/km	100%
CO_2 emissions between 76 and 130 g/km	18%
CO_2 emissions over 130 g/km	8%
Energy efficient and water saving plant	
First year allowance	100%

Capital gains

Annual exempt amount	£11,100
Standard rate (residential property/other disposals)	18/10%
Higher rate (residential property/other disposals)	28/20%
Entrepreneur's relief rate	10%
Entrepreneurs' relief limit	£10,000,000

National Insurance rates

Class 2 contributions:	£2.80 per week
Small earnings exemption	£5,965 p.a.
Class 4 contributions:	
Main rate	9%
Additional rate	2%
Lower earnings limit	£8,060
Upper earnings limit	£43,000

Corporation tax

Financial year	2016	2015
All profits and gains	20%	20%

Introduction to business tax

Administration

- Taxation administered by HM Revenue & Customs (HMRC).

- Rules covering tax are contained in statute (law) which is passed every year (Finance Act).

- Decisions reached by the courts interpreting the law are known as case law.

- HMRC also issue guidance – Extra Statutory Concessions and Statements of Practice.

Taxes

- Corporation Tax – paid by companies on both income and capital gains.

- Income Tax – paid by individuals on their income.

- Capital Gains Tax – paid by individuals on their capital gains.

Tax avoidance and tax evasion

- Tax evasion
  Any action taken to evade tax by illegal means; this carries a risk of criminal prosecution.
  Examples of tax evasion include failing to declare income and claiming false expenses.

- Tax avoidance
  Use of legitimate means to minimise taxpayer's tax liability, for example by investing in a tax-free ISA (Individual Savings Account).

Adjustment of profits – sole traders, partnerships and companies

Pro forma for adjustment of profits

	£	£
Net profit as per accounts		X
Add: Expenses charged in the accounts that are not allowable as trading expenses	X	
		X
		X
Less: Income included in the accounts which is not assessable as trading income	X	
		(X)
Adjusted profit/(loss)		X

Disallowed expenses

- Expenses that fail the remoteness test so not "wholly and exclusively" for trading purposes.

- Fines on the business or fraud by directors/owners.

- Donations to national charities – might be allowed as a charge on income if Gift Aid donations. Political donations are never allowable.

- Capital expenditure, e.g. purchase of equipment included in profit and loss account.

- Depreciation. Capital allowances granted instead.

- Costs of bringing newly acquired second-hand assets to useable condition.

- Legal and professional expenses relating to capital items or breaking the law.

- Customer entertaining. Staff entertaining can be allowable.

- Customer gifts, unless gift incorporates business advertising, cost is less than £50 per annum per customer, and gift is not food, drink, tobacco or cash vouchers.

Non-assessable income

- Income taxed in any other way, e.g. interest or property income for individuals.

- Profits on sale of fixed assets.

Unincorporated businesses – trading income

Trading income calculated for each period of account:

	£
Adjusted accounting profit	X
Less: Capital allowances:	
Plant and machinery	(X)
Plus: Balancing charges	X
Trading income for the period of account	X

Expenses charged in the accounts which are not allowable as trading expenses

- See adjustment of profits – sole traders, partnerships and companies
- Transactions with the owner of the business. For example:
    - Add back salary paid to owner. Salaries paid to family members do not need to be added back.
    - Private expenditure included in accounts.
    - Class 2 National Insurance contributions.
    - Goods taken for own use.

Private use assets
- Private use assets have separate column in Capital Allowance computation.
- Disallow private use % of WDA/AIA/FYA.

Capital allowances – business cessation
- In the cessation period of account, no WDA/AIA/FYA.
- Include additions and disposals as normal. Any asset taken over by owner, treat as a disposal at market value. Balancing adjustment made (balancing charge or balancing allowance).

Sole traders – basis periods

Tax year – 2016/17 tax year runs from 6 April 2016 to 5 April 2017

Basis period rules
- First year – runs from start date of trading to the next 5 April.
- Second year and third year:

```
                                    ┌─────────────────┐
                                    │ Is there a      │
                                    │ period of       │
                  ──── Yes ─────────┤ account          ├──── No ────┐
                 │                  │ ending in the   │            │
                 │                  │ second tax      │            │
                 │                  │ year?           │            │
                 │                  └─────────────────┘            │
                 │                                        ┌──────────────────┐
          ┌──────────────┐                                │ Basis period runs │
          │ How long is  │                                │ from 6 April to 5 │
          │ the period   │                                │ April in second   │
          │ of account?  │                                │ tax year.         │
          └──────────────┘                                └──────────────────┘
```

12 months	Less than 12 months	More than 12 months
Basis period is that period of account	Basis period is first 12 months of trade	Basis period is 12 months to the accounting date in second tax year

```
                        Third tax year
```

CYB	CYB	CYB

Basis period is 12 months to the accounting date in the third tax year

Later years – basis period is the period of account ending in the tax year = Current Year basis (CYB).

Final year – basis period is the period from the end of the basis period for the previous tax year to cessation date.

Overlap profits - opening year rules may lead to profits being taxed twice. Relief is given on cessation of the business.

Sole traders – change of accounting date

For an accounting date change to be recognised for tax purposes the following conditions must be satisfied:

- The first accounts ending on the new date must not exceed 18 months in length.

- The sole trader or partnership must give notice of the change in the tax return by the filing date of the tax return.

"Year of change" – is the first tax year in which accounts are made up to the new date.

"Relevant period" – is the time to the new accounting date from the end of the previous basis period.

Example 1 – relevant period is less than 12 months

Jasmin changes her accounting date as follows:

Accounts	Year	Basis period
Year to 31 December 2014	2014/15	1/1/14 to 31/12/14
9 months to 30 September 2015	2015/16	1/10/14 to 30/9/15
Year to 30 September 2016	2016/17	1/10/15 to 30/9/16

Year of change – 2015/16
Relevant period – 9 months to 30 September 2015

Example 2 – relevant period is greater than 12 months

Vaughan changes his accounting date as follows:

Accounts	Year	Basis period
Year to 31 December 2014	2014/15	1/1/14 to 31/12/14
15 months to 31 March 2016	2015/16	1/1/15 to 31/3/16
Year to 31 March 2017	2016/17	1/4/16 to 31/3/17

Year of change – 2015/16
Relevant period – 15 months to 31 March 2016

The rules for determining basis periods on a change of accounting date are complex. Significant examples of changes in accounting dates are:

- after the 3rd year of trading,
- with accounts of 18 months or less, and
- not straddling a tax year.

Capital allowances on plant and machinery

Layout of capital allowances on plant and machinery computation

(see taxation tables for rates)

	First Year Allowance (FYA)	Annual Investment Allowance(AIA)	General pool	Special rate pool	Short Life Asset	Total allowances
	£	£	£	£	£	£
WDV b/f			X	X	X	
Additions	X	X	X			
Disposals			(X)		(X)	
	—	—	—	—	—	
	X	X	X	X	X	
Balancing allowance/balancing charge(BA/BC)					X/(X)	X/(X)
					—	
					Nil	
AIA/FYA	(X)	(X)				X
Writing down allowance@ 18% pa			(X)			X
Writing down allowance@ 8% pa	—	—	—	(X)		X
				—		
WDV c/f	Nil ===	Nil ===	X ===	X ===		—
Total allowances						X ===

- Plant – defined by 'function/setting' distinction and case law.
- AIA – 100% allowance for expenditure (other than cars) in 12 month period (pro rata). Expenditure in excess of AIA qualifies for writing down allowance (WDA).
- Full WDA for the period is given regardless of date of purchase of item. WDA is scaled for periods other than 12 months.
- FYA – 100% allowance given on purchase of environmentally friendly cars and energy saving/water efficient plant. FYA is not scaled for short accounting periods.
- If the written down value (WDV) on the general pool (= WDV b/f + additions-disposals) is £1,000 or less then pool is written off as small pools annual writing down allowance.
- Short life assets (SLA) – de-pool asset if life expected to be less than 8 years. Not available for cars.

Partnerships

- Each partner is taxed like a sole trader on their share of the partnership profits

- First step is to share accounting profits between partners:
  - Allocate the correct salaries and interest on capital for the period to each partner.

  - Divide the remaining profit for each set of accounts between the partners based upon the profit sharing arrangement.

  - You may need to split the period if there is a change such as a partner joining or leaving.

- Opening year and cessation rules apply to partners individually when they join or leave the partnership.

- Allocate the profit for each partner to the correct tax year using usual basis period rules.

- Basis periods for continuing partners are unaffected by joiners or leavers.

- Each partner enters their share of profits for a tax year in the partnership pages of their own tax return.

Trading losses for sole traders and partners

- A loss is computed in the same way as a profit, making the same adjustments to the net profit as per the accounts and deducting capital allowances.

Set off of trading loss against total income

- Set off loss against total income of the preceding tax year and/or the tax year of loss, e.g. loss in 2016/17 set off against total income in 2015/16 and/or 2016/17.

- Cannot restrict loss to preserve use of personal allowance so personal allowance may be wasted.

- For 2016/17 loss claim needed by 31 January 2019.

Carry forward of trading losses

- If any loss remains unrelieved after current year and carry back claim has been made, or no such claims are made, then carry forward the loss against first available profits of the same trade.

Choice of loss relief – consider the following:

- Utilize loss in the tax year in which income is taxed at a higher rate.

- Possible wastage of personal allowance.

- Review the projected future profits to ensure the loss can be utilised.

- If cash flow is important, a loss carry back claim may result in a tax refund being paid to the company.

Payment and administration – sole traders and partners

The return must be filed by:
- 31 October following the end of the tax year if filing a paper return.

- 31 January following the end of the tax year if filing online.

Penalties for late filing and payment

Late filing	Late payment	Penalty
Miss filing deadline		£100
	30 days late	5% of tax due or £300, if greater
3 months late		Daily penalty £10 per day for up to 90 days (max £900)
6 months late		5% of tax due or £300, if greater
	6 months late	5% of tax outstanding at that date
12 months late		5% or £300 if greater
	12 months late	5% of tax outstanding at that date
12 months and information deliberately withheld		Based on behaviour: • deliberate and concealed withholding 100% of tax due, or £300 if greater. • deliberate but not concealed 70% of tax due, or £300 if greater. Reductions of up to half of the above %'s apply for cooperation with investigation.

Disclosure and errors

- Taxpayer must notify HMRC by 5 October following end of the tax year if a tax return is needed.
- Taxpayer can amend a tax return within 12 months of filing date or make an error or mistake claim within 3 years of the filing date.

Payments on account (POA)

- Due 31 January (in tax year) and 31 July (after tax year end). Each instalment is 50% of the previous year's tax and Class 4 National Insurance contribution (NIC) liability.
- Balancing payment made 31 January after tax year end.
- No POA due if last year's tax and Class 4 NIC liability less than £1,000 or greater than 80% if last year's liability was deducted at source.
- Can reduce POA if this year's liability expected to be less than last year's. Penalties will be charged if a deliberate incorrect claim is made.
- Capital gains tax (CGT) liability is paid 31 January following the tax year end. No POA needed for CGT.

Interest on tax paid late/overpaid tax

- Interest charged daily on late payment.

Enquiries and other penalties

- HMRC must notify individual of enquiry within 12 months of submission of return.
- Basis of enquiry – random or HMRC believe income/expenses misstated.
- Penalty for failure to produce enquiry documents = £50 + £30 per day.
- Penalty for failure to keep proper records is up to £3,000. Records must be kept for 5 years after the filing date for the relevant tax year.
- Penalties for incorrect returns are:

Type of behaviour	Maximum	Unprompted (minimum)	Prompted (minimum)
Genuine mistake: despite taking reasonable care	0%	0%	0%
Careless error and inaccuracy is due to failure to take reasonable care	30%	0%	15%
Deliberate error but not concealed	70%	20%	35%
Deliberate error and concealed	100%	30%	50%

National Insurance contributions

- Self-employed individuals pay Class 2 and Class 4 contributions.

  Class 4 contributions are at 9% on profits between the lower and upper limits, then 2% on profits above the upper limit.

- Percentages and limits are provided in the Taxation Tables.

An outline of corporation tax

- Companies pay corporation tax on their profits for each accounting period.

- There is one rate of corporation tax set each financial year.

- Profits = Income + Gains – Charges

- Accounting periods are usually 12 months long but can be shorter.

- If a company's accounts are longer than 12 months, the first 12 months will be one accounting period and the remainder a second accounting period.

- All UK property income is pooled as a single source of income and taxed on an accruals basis.

- Borrowing or lending money by a company is a loan relationship.

- Trading loan relationships are part of trading income.

- Non-trading loan relationships (NTL-R) are pooled to give NTL-R credits or deficits.

- Gift Aid donations are charges on income.

- Associated companies – a company is associated with another if one company controls the other or they are both controlled by the same 'person'.

The calculation of total profits and corporation tax payable

ABC Ltd

Corporation tax computation for the year/period ended DD/MM/20XX

	£
Trading income – accruals basis	X
Interest income – accrual basis	X
Property income – accruals basis	X
Chargeable gains	X
	X
Less charges on income – Gift Aid donations	(X)
Total profits	X
Corporation tax payable – Total profits × Corporation tax rate	X

Key points

- Trading income is adjusted from net profit per company accounts less capital allowances.
- All income in computation to be gross.
- Some income may need to be grossed up. Companies receive interest gross.
- Virtually all interest receivable is taxed as interest income.
- Dividends payable by a company are not an allowable expense.
- UK dividends receivable by a company are not taxable.
- Net-off current year capital losses against current year capital gains. If there is a net capital loss carry it forward.
- See taxation tables for corporation tax rates.

Non 31 March year-ends
- For example – year ended 31 December 2016. 3 months of period falls in financial year 2015 (FY15) and 9 months in FY16.
- Apportion Total Profits to FY. Apply correct tax rate for FY.

Long periods of account
- Will consist of two accounting periods = first 12 months and remainder of period.
- Split profits as follows:
  - Adjusted trading profit and property income – time apportion.
  - Capital allowances – separate computations for each CAP.
  - Interest income – accruals basis.
  - Chargeable gains – according to date of disposal.
  - Charges on income – according to date paid.

Corporation tax – losses

- Can elect to set trading losses against current accounting period total profits. Gift aid donations (charges) will remain unrelieved.

- If the above election is made, can also carry back trading loss to set against total profits within the previous 12 months.

- Trading losses are automatically carried forward to set against the first available profits of the same trade if not utilised by the above two claims.

- If there is a choice of loss relief, firstly consider the rate of loss relief then the timing of relief.

- Set out the use of the losses in a loss memorandum.

Corporation tax – payment and administration

Payment dates
- Small companies (annual profits less than £1.5 million): 9 months + 1 day after end of the accounting period (CAP).

- Large companies (annual profits greater than £1.5 million) must estimate year's tax liability and pay 25% of the year's liability:
    - 6 months and 14 days after start of CAP
    - 9 months and 14 days after start of CAP
    - 14 days after end of CAP
    - 3 months and 14 days after end of CAP

- Estimate must be revised for each quarter. Penalties may be charged if company deliberately fails to pay sufficient instalments.

- No instalments due for first year company is large unless profits are greater than £10 million.

- Associated companies share the annual profit limit of £1.5 million equally.

Interest on late payments
- Interest charged daily on late payment. Overpayment of tax receives interest from HMRC. Interest is taxable/tax allowable as interest income.

Filing the return
- Filed on the later of 12 months after end of CAP or 3 months after the notice to deliver a tax return has been issued.

- Late filing penalties are: less than 3 months late: £100; greater than 3 months late: £200; greater than 6 months late: 10% of tax due per return; greater than 12 months late: 20% of tax due per return.

- Company must notify HMRC it is within scope of corporation tax within 3 months of starting to trade.

- Company can amend return within 12 months of the filing date.

Enquiries and other penalties
- HMRC must notify company of enquiry within 12 months of submission of return.

- Basis of enquiry – random or HMRC believe income/expenses misstated.

- Penalty for failure to produce enquiry documents: £50 + £30 per day.

- Penalty for failure to keep proper records is up to £3,000. Records must be retained for six years after the end of the relevant accounting period.

- Penalties for incorrect returns are the same as for sole traders and partners – see sole traders and partners link.

Current tax reliefs and other tax issues

Research and Development (R&D) Tax Credits for Small and Medium Sized Companies

A small or medium sized enterprise (SME) is a company with less than 500 employees with either:
- an annual turnover under €100 million, or
- a balance sheet under €86 million.

The SME tax relief scheme

From 1 April 2015, the tax relief on allowable R&D costs is 230%.

R&D tax credits

If a company makes a loss, it can choose to receive R&D tax credits instead of carrying forward a loss. The amount of tax credit is limited to the total of PAYE and National Insurance contribution liabilities of the company.

Costs that qualify for R&D tax relief

To qualify as R&D, any activity must contribute directly to seeking an advance in science or technology or must be a qualifying indirect activity.

Intermediaries (IR35) legislation

IR35 legislation prevents personal service companies ("PSC") being used to disguise permanent employment.

The rules apply where the relationship between the worker and the client, would be considered to be an employment relationship if the existence of the PSC was ignored.

If the rules apply, a **deemed employment income tax charge** is charged on the PSC.

The **deemed employment income tax charge** is calculated based upon the actual payments made to the PSC by the client.

Introduction to chargeable gains

- Individual pays Capital Gains Tax (CGT) on net chargeable gains in a tax year.

- For companies, chargeable gains are included as income in calculating total profits.

- Individuals receive an annual exempt amount from CGT – for 2016/17 this is £11,100.

- Gains/losses arise when a chargeable person makes a chargeable disposal of a chargeable asset.

- Chargeable person – individual or company.

- Chargeable disposal – sale, gift or loss/destruction of the whole or part of an asset.
  Exempt disposals – on death and gifts to approved charities.

- Chargeable asset – all assets unless exempt. Exempt assets are motor cars and some chattels.

Calculation of capital gains tax

Net chargeable gains – total gains in the tax year after netting off any current year or brought forward losses and the annual exempt amount.

Annual exempt amount (AE)

- For individuals only.

- AE cannot be carried forward or carried back.

- Current year losses must be netted off against current year gains before AE. This means AE can be wasted.

- Brought forward capital losses are set off against current year gains after AE so AE is not wasted.

Calculation of gains and losses for individuals

Pro forma computation

	£	£
Consideration received		X
Less Incidental costs of sale		(X)
Net sale proceeds		NSP
Less Allowable expenditure		
- Acquisition cost	X	
- Incidental costs of acquisition	X	
- Enhancement expenditure	X	
		(Cost)
Gain/(Loss)		X/(X)

- Consideration received is usually sales proceeds, but market value will be used instead of actual consideration where the transaction is a gift or between connected persons.

- An individual is connected with their spouse, lineal relatives (and their spouses) and spouse's relatives (and their spouses).

- Husband and wife/civil partner transfers – nil gain nil loss. Tax planning opportunity.

Part disposals – the cost allocated to the disposal = Cost × (A/(A+B))

A = consideration received on part disposal   B = market value of the remainder of the asset

Chattels - tangible moveable object. Two types:

- Wasting – expected life of 50 years or less (e.g. racehorse or boat). CGT exempt.
  Non-wasting – expected life greater than 50 years (e.g. antiques or jewellery).

CGT, £6,000 rule

Buy Sell	£6,000 or less	More than £6,000
Less than £6,000	Exempt	Allowable loss but proceeds are deemed = £6,000
More than £6,000	Normal calculation of the gain, then compare with 5/3(gross proceeds - £6,000) - Take the lower gain	Chargeable in full

Shares and securities – disposals by individuals

CGT on shares and securities

Disposal of shares and securities are subject to CGT except for listed government securities (gilt-edged securities or 'gilts'), qualifying corporate bonds (e.g. company loan notes/debentures) and shares held in an Individual Savings Account (ISA).

The identification rules

Used to determine which shares have been sold and so what acquisition cost can be deducted from the sale proceeds (e.g. match the disposal and acquisition).

Disposals are matched:

- Firstly, with acquisitions on the same day as the day of disposal.

- Secondly, with acquisitions made in the 30 days following the date of disposal (FIFO basis).

- Thirdly, with shares from the share pool.

The Share Pool

- The share pool contains all shares acquired prior to the disposal date.

- Each acquisition is not kept separately, but is 'pooled' together with other acquisitions and a running total kept of the number of shares and the cost of those shares.

- When a disposal from the pool is made, the appropriate number of shares are taken from the pool along with the average cost of those shares.

- The gain on disposal is then calculated.

Bonus issues and rights issues

- Bonus issue – no adjustment to cost needed.
- Rights issue – adjustment to cost needed.

Chargeable gains – reliefs available to individuals

Replacement of business assets (Rollover) relief – when a qualifying business asset is sold at a gain, taxpayer can defer gain by reinvesting proceeds in a qualifying replacement asset.

- Deferred gain is deducted from the cost of the replacement asset so gain crystallises when the replacement asset is sold.

- Qualifying assets (original and replacement) – must be used in a trade by the vendor and be land and buildings, fixed plant and machinery or goodwill.

- Qualifying time period – replacement asset must be purchased between 1 year before and 3 years after the sale of the original asset.

- Partial reinvestment – only some of the sales proceeds reinvested then the gain taxable is the lower of the full gain and the proceeds not reinvested.

Gift relief (holdover relief) – donee takes over asset at donor's base cost i.e. the gain is given away along with the asset.

- Qualifying assets – trade assets of donor or shares in any unquoted trading company or personal trading company (individual owns at least 5% of company).

Entrepreneurs' relief – gain taxable at 10% capital gains tax rate.

- The £10 million limit is a lifetime limit which is reduced each time a claim for the relief is made.

- For 2016/17 claim must be made by 31 January 2019.

- Qualifying business disposals (assets must be owned for at least 12 months prior to sale)

  - The whole or part of a business carried on by the individual (alone or in partnership).

  - Assets of the individual's or partnership's trading business that has now ceased.

  - Shares in the individual's 'personal trading company'. Individual must have owned the shares and been an employee of the company for 12 months prior to sale.

- From 17 March 2016, newly issued shares in unlisted trading companies purchased on or after 17 March 2016 by external investors qualify for entrepreneurs' relief provided they are continually held for a minimum of 3 years from 6 April 2016.

Calculation of gains and losses for companies

Pro forma computation

	£	£
Consideration received		X
Less Incidental costs of sale		(X)
Net sale proceeds		NSP
Less Allowable expenditure		
Acquisition cost + incidental costs of acquisition	X	
Indexation allowance [indexation factor × expenditure]	X	
Enhancement expenditure	X	
Indexation allowance	X	
		(Cost)
Chargeable gain		Gain

- Indexation allowance is not available where there is an unindexed loss; nor can it turn an unindexed gain into an indexed loss.

- Note that companies do not get an annual exempt amount.

- Losses relieved in order – current year first followed by losses brought forward.

Only relief available to companies is rollover relief:

- Rollover relief is a deferral relief – see [Chargeable gains – reliefs available to individuals] for main rollover relief rules.
- Key differences applying for companies:
    - Indexation is given on disposal of the original asset.
    - Goodwill is not a qualifying asset for companies.
    - Gain deferred is the indexed gain.
    - On disposal of the replacement asset, indexation is calculated on the 'base cost' not actual cost.

Shares and securities – disposals by companies

The identification rules - a disposal of shares is matched:

- firstly, with same-day transactions
- secondly, with transactions in the previous 9 days (FIFO). No indexation allowance is available
- thirdly, with shares from the 1985 pool (shares bought from 1 April 1982 onwards).

1985 pool – pro forma working	No.	Cost £	Indexed cost £
Purchase	X	X	X
Index to next operative event			X
			X
Operative event (purchase)	X	X	X
	X	X	X
Index to next operative event			X
			X
Operative event (sale)	(X)	(X)	(X)A
Pool carried forward	X	X	X

Operative event = purchase, sale, rights issue. Bonus issue is not an operative event.

Computation

	£
Proceeds	X
Less indexed cost (A from pool)	(X)
Indexed gain	X

The badges of trade

6 Badges of Trade

- Subject matter
- Ownership
- Frequency of transactions
- Improvement expenditure
- Reason for sale
- Motive for profit

Duties and responsibilities of a tax adviser

- Maintain client confidentiality at all times.

- AAT members must adopt an ethical approach and maintain an objective outlook.

- Give timely and constructive advice to clients.

- Honest and professional conduct with HMRC

- A tax advisor is liable to a £3,000 penalty if they assist in making an incorrect return.

for your notes

for your notes

for your notes

for your notes

for your notes

for your notes

for your notes

for your notes

_____